The Great Television Series

The Great Television Series

Jeff Rovin

South Brunswick and New York: A. S. Barnes and Company

London: Thomas Yoseloff Ltd

© 1977 by A. S. Barnes and Co., Inc.

A. S. Barnes and Co., Inc.
Cranbury, New Jersey 08512

Thomas Yoseloff Ltd
Magdalen House
136-148 Tooley Street
London SE1 2TT, England

Library of Congress Cataloging in Publication Data

Rovin, Jeff.
  The great television series.

  Includes index.
  1. Television programs—United States—History.
I. Title.
PN1992.3.U5R68 1977   791.45′7   76-50213
ISBN 0-498-01961-6

PRINTED IN THE UNITED STATES OF AMERICA

Contents

Acknowledgments

The author would like to thank Brad Franklin, Tom A. Jones of Walt Disney Productions, Vic Ghidalia of ABC, Michael G. Silver of CBS, and Paula Klaw of *Movie Star News* for contributing photographs to this volume. Special thanks to Roger Youman for permission to reprint select passages of interviews that appeared in *TV Guide* magazine and to Geraldine Duclow of the Philadelphia Free Library Theatre Collection.

Introduction

The death of television's Superman, George Reeves, was a shock and a puzzle to his millions of adolescent followers. For seven years, youngsters across the nation had watched rifle shells bounce off his body, and knives bend like rubber against his chest. How could a single bullet stop "The Man of Steel"? The answer was apparent only as his fans grew older and came to understand the reality of television. Like motion pictures, TV is an act, a play brought to our homes by electronic gadgetry. It caricatures our values and life-styles, exaggerating reality for comedic or dramatic truth. Paradoxically, however, television is not a sham.

Now, as in the fifties, picture tubes are comparatively small, the action is contrived to fit predetermined time slots, and the screen image is hazy when compared with theatrical motion pictures. Yet, viewers gather around their TV sets religiously because it's a *personal* medium.

It not only involves an audience in a character's life, but it brings him on a weekly visit into one's bedroom or den. This makes him an intimate, if distant, friend.

In its twenty-nine-year history, television has seen hundreds of series come and go, and among this vast repertoire we have our favorite motifs. Variety shows have always been plentiful, as have cartoon programs; situation comedies, game shows, soap operas, and cramped theatrical movies abound. However, of them all, the television hero—be he a policeman, cowboy, or physician—holds a warm and nostalgic place in our hearts. Let us look, then, at *The Great Television Series*. We'll trace their development from the gods of the fifties to the fallen angels of the seventies, and make some predictions as to his future in the medium. Significantly, by watching the hero and his video evolution, perhaps we'll also learn something about ourselves.

The Great Television Series

1

The Six Inch Hero

A hero differs from other men in the degree of his powers.

—*Scholar C. M. Bowra*

It seems a paradox to say that television does justice to a hero. A picture tube is less than two feet long diagonally, and it reduces even moon rockets or film spectaculars to a small square of light. How can such a medium possibly accommodate a figure that, by definition, must be larger than life? The answer lies in the medium's unique combination of visuals, familiarity, and variety.

Literature and radio, both, can paint tapestries as sweeping as their creators desire, for they enact their tales in the theater of the mind. But there is nothing so powerful as a picture. Film has the money and giant screen to present a Douglas Fairbanks, Sr. or John Wayne in all their rough-and-tumble glory. But you see the actor for only ninety minutes every six months or so—a showcase that requires years to build a heroic image. Television is different. In the same way that one gets to know a political leader or a sports figure from daily news accounts, one becomes familiar with the television hero. His dimension comes through repetition, exposure to a new and different menace every week. Ironically, then, television is perhaps the medium best equipped to serve as a stage for the hero. And it has done so ever since programming was undertaken in earnest.

Although television had been in existence for twenty-three years, there wasn't a concerted effort to create regular entertainment series until after the war. Within two years, television had started broadcasting other than news events, at which time a phenomenal and geometric climb began: there were 7,500 sets in 1932; 14,000 by 1947; 190,000 by 1949; 5,000,000 by 1950; and 50,000,000 by 1960. This last increase is an average jump of ten thousand sets daily!

Many of the television heroes at whom we'll be looking in this chapter owe a great debt to their antecedents— the movie-serial heroes. The serials were sprawling adventure sagas that packed motion-picture houses for weekend matinees. Twelve to fifteen episodes comprised a complete serial, and they dominated children's film fare from 1929 to 1952. The mode lingered on for another four years, but the competition from television was too great. Theatrical receipts overall took a dramatic thirty percent plunge—from 76,000,000 to 50,000,000 paid admissions per week—and the serials were discontinued altogether. Fortunately, as we'll see later in the chapter, many of the serial actors were able to find work in television; in fact, a number of early shows were simply weekly or even daily broadcasts of the action-filled chapter plays! Conceptually, however, the serial hero was a prototype of these early heroes created especially for television. Both were on display for nearly a half-hour every week, faced new dangers in each episode of a continuing saga, and due to limited budgets and hasty production schedules were saddled with cardboard sets, very straightforward, uninventive photography, and little time for rehearsal. The difference was that television, unlike the movie serial, distinguished between adult and

William Boyd as Hopalong Cassidy, astride his horse Topper.

16

juvenile broadcasts. The serial offshoots created for home viewing were for the kids, while the after-7:00 P.M. fare was generally for their parents. Of course, in 1948, there wasn't much of a selection in either category. In addition to local programs that featured edited theatrical films or sports events, the radio networks that had moved into television offered variety shows such as "The Original Amateur Hour," "Toast of the Town," with Ed Sullivan, and "Texaco Star Theatre," with Milton Berle; game shows like "Winner Take All," hosted by radio's Superman Bud Collyer, or "Break the Bank," with Bert Parks; and the dramatic anthology programs "Philco Playhouse" and "Studio One," where such stars as Jack Lemmon and Charlton Heston first received widespread public recognition. As for heroes, the first ones unveiled by television were a pair of cowboys, as Hopalong Cassidy and the Lone Ranger thundered across the picture tube. It was only natural that these two properties inaugurated television's action programming, since over half of the screen's 232 serials were Westerns.

The first "Hopalong Cassidy" TV shows were simply condensed versions of the sixty-six feature-length films. These Paramount productions originally went before the cameras in 1935 with a thirty-seven-year-old actor from Cambridge, Ohio, in the title role. His name was William Boyd, and astride the durable steed Topper— who was with Boyd for all the Hoppy films—he faced such foreboding menaces as *The Eagle's Brood* (1935), *Forty Thieves* (1945), and *The Devil's Playground* (1946). What distinguished Boyd from such contemporary Western players as Ken Maynard or Roy Rogers was that he was mature, low-keyed, and basically nonviolent, although the films always concluded with a rousing reel of action. This was certainly a far cry from what author Clarence E. Mulford had envisioned Hoppy to be: a slight, limping, mustachioed, tobacco-chewing, and unkempt cowpoke. Nonetheless, the Boyd interpretation was extremely popular, and production of the theatrical films continued until 1951—that's when Boyd began producing, as well as starring, in adventures created especially for television. These escapades were considerably less explosive than the movies, even sporting such comparatively tame titles as "Hidden Gold" and "Border Vigilante." But they brought Hoppy new popularity, for he was available to the public at the flick of a switch and in the comfort of their own homes. However, Boyd felt that there was another reason for his success in this new medium:

Kids are smarter and better developed today than they were eighteen years ago. Consequently, Hoppy has to keep up with their intelligence. He, too, is a little sharper, and not so much a corny philosopher. He thinks a little quicker now, and talks faster. Besides, you can't get an audience to watch a three or four minute fight now: they know that two men can't absorb that much punishment and live. Now we just exchange a few blows and get it over with.

The late actor also understood the power of a hero figure, and had definite opinions about the bent of the programs he was presenting on television:

At one time, action was most important in a western, but that isn't true today. I try to get a lesson for kids in each story. I show them the difference between good and bad. It's much easier to demonstrate than tell.

Keeping Hoppy company in 1948 was the Lone Ranger, a character whose sincerity was absolute and his devotion to humanity unflappable. Unlike the Boyd hero, whose career began in print, the Lone Ranger, brother of Capt. Dan Reid of the Texas Rangers, was a character created for radio. The sole survivor of an ambush worked by the notorious Butch Cavendish, the lawman was found and nursed to health by an Indian named Tonto. And, since Reid wished to perpetuate the front of his death, he made a mask from the black vest that had belonged to his brother—another victim of the massacre—and became the mysterious Lone Ranger, a symbol of justice in the old West. To Tonto, who remained as his sidekick, he was "Kemo Sabay," or "Trusted Friend," the white man who, as a boy, had saved the Indian's life.

"The Lone Ranger" premiered on California radio station WXYZ on 30 January 1933, the brainchild of station owner George Trendle and writer Fran Striker. He was an immediate success and reached the movies in *The Lone Ranger* (1938), a fifteen-chapter serial starring Lee Powell. A year later, *The Lone Ranger Rides Again* was released, with Bob Livingston in the lead. On television, Clayton Moore was the first actor to don the lawman's black mask. Moore, a veteran of nine serials, had gained his greatest recognition prior to "The Lone Ranger" as archaeologist Larry Grayson in the popular serial "The Perils of Nyoka" (1942). After three seasons—seventy-eight episodes—he turned in his silver bullets and John Hart assumed the role. Hart's tenure lasted a pair of twenty-six-show seasons, after which the program went from network to syndicated reruns.[1] TV's Tonto was Jay Silverheels, born in Ontario, Canada's Six Nations Indian Reservation, a full-blooded Mohawk by birth. Silverheels stayed in buckskins for the entire five-year run of the show.

As a hero, the Lone Ranger combined the best of the Western with all the swash of a popular comic-book

The Lone Ranger (Clayton Moore) and Silver.

character. He could fight, rope, and shoot, and did so with all the dramatic flair of a Batman-gone-Laramie! Perhaps the prime example of this occurred in one episode when, riding his horse Silver at full gallop, the Lone Ranger thundered into a lawless town, saw a mob about to lynch Tonto, and from several hundred yards away split the rope with a single shot. Hastening to the Indian's side, he helped him onto Silver and sped away before anyone knew what had happened. And the Masked Man used his head on occasion, as well! Once when an outlaw tried to corner the Ranger in a house, Reid found a full-length mirror that, when strategically placed, reflected his image, fooled the pursuer, and ultimately led to his capture. At other times, Kemo Sabay sallied forth in disguise, his favorites being that of an old prospector, a grizzled Union officer, the smooth-talking medicine man Prof. Horatio Tucker, the Mexican bandit Jose, a red-headed Irish-Mexican patriot known as Don Pedro O'Sullivan, and a hulking Swede.

Of course, not only did the Ranger have to fulfill the requisite deeds of any hero; on first appearance, everyone naturally assumed that the Masked Man was a bandit, so he also had to overperform just to win their confidence! However, after the shock of his disguise had been dulled by a successful campaign against the outlaws at hand, the Long Ranger evidenced the prime virtue of any good hero—the temperance of modesty—by always vanishing before he could be thanked or congratulated. This left those whom he had helped to wonder aloud—as much for posterity as their own illumination—"Who *was* that Masked Man?"

This dramatic thread notwithstanding, the interesting thing about the Lone Ranger was his lack of a message. In this respect, he was quite unlike Boyd's Hopalong Cassidy or our next featured hero, both of whom always had something to say in the form of a fable or sermon, respectively. "The Long Ranger" was simply an unpretentious adventure series in which the good guys always won—period. Whatever message a viewer drew from the show was up to him. This lack of forthright moral commentary moved some early TV critics to complain that the medium was evil, simply a showcase for violent action—a debate that rages to this day. Then, as now, this was nonsense.

Forming a saddle-bound triumverate in 1948 was "The Ghost Rider," the masked host of a Philadelphia-based program that featured old theatrical Westerns. There were accoutrements that viewers could buy to become members of The Ghost Rider Club, but beyond its entertainment value the program defended television from the educators and parents who felt that it was a bad influence on children. They felt that young viewers might be wrongly inspired to emulate the struggles and fisti-cuffs of their small-screen heroes. Accordingly, "The Ghost Rider" was initiated as an afternoon program and designed, as per its press releases, "to use the over-whelming influence the cowboy hero has on the mind of any youngster and use it as a force for good." Ironically, according to industry observers, youngsters followed the Ghost Rider's suggestions for right and proper behavior more religiously than they did when these same comments were issued from teachers or parents.[2]

The number of action programs climbed from three to seven in 1949. Joining "The Ghost Rider" in the afternoon—or airing in prime time,[3] depending on the city—was a radical departure from the Western, the legendary science-fiction hero Captain Video. Also referred to as The Electronic Wizard—commensurate with one's intimacy to the space ranger—Captain Video was played by the jut-jawed Al Hodge, a performer of varied experience who, among his other accomplish-ments, had been the voice of the Green Hornet on the radio. This flashy space opera was broadcast for a half-hour daily, and had our hero rocketing about the earth with his Video Rangers to battle such bad men as Dr. Pauli and his evil ilk. To this end, Capt. Video included in his arsenal such popular weapons as the

Talk-show host Mike Douglas (left) and Al Hodge on a 1975 "Mike Douglas Show." They are shown taking the Video Ranger Pledge.

Cosmic Ray Vibrator, which caused an antagonist to shake until he was exhausted, and the Thermoid Ejector, a gun that fired infrared thermal currents.

While Capt. Video's courageous astronautics made him an idol to the young, the fact that he was run through with the moral fiber of Al Hodge also made him, like Hopalong Cassidy, a spokesman for practical excel-lence. There was more to the hero than just the fortitude that comes from wielding a Cosmic Ray Vibrator. Hodge was a Sunday-school teacher in Manhasset, Long Island, and explained at the time:

Every week, without fail, I see several new faces in class. At the end of each session, I notice that the newcomers have been taken aside and, in hushed whispers, learn that I am *Capt. Video* himself. The identification does have a very good aspect. At least three times a week on *Capt. Video*, we deliver short messages to our youthful listeners. We stress the Golden Rule, tolerance, honesty, and personal integri-ty. I'm thankful for the opportunity of being associated with the show that helps, in a small measure, to illuminate for the young people of America, the importance of courage, character, and the sense of moral values.

Unfortunately, "Capt. Video" was the only new program that went out of its way to allow the nobler bent of the hero to dominate the story. The other series, although they were about "men in armor," seldom showed them as knights. Of course, "Martin Kane: Private Eye" and "Man Against Crime" were adult efforts, so our perspective must be altered somewhat. No longer are we dealing with preachers, but avenging angels, men who execute the law rather than pontificate about its merits.[4]

"Martin Kane," a late-night entry, was a program that specialized in surprise endings. The pipe-smoking character came to television from radio and retained all of his dead-pan intensity in the translation. He was a detective who put business before all else; the only women with whom he was ever involved were those who employed the free-lance private eye. Even then, there was never any romantic attachment; not so much as a suggestive remark or a "thank-you" kiss. And the first man to play the gumshoe captured this asceticism with precision. William Gargan, who had played Ellery Queen in the movies, had actually been a detective before he became an actor and thus brought authority to the role. Unfortunately, he left the show in 1951 to become a producer and was succeeded by Lloyd Nolan. Nolan, a veteran of seventy-five theatrical films, was thrilled with the assignment, saying that "Martin Kane is the kind of quiet, calculating character I genuinely love to play." But Nolan's staid demeanor was only skin deep, and after two seasons he handed the part to Lee Tracy, a more somber film actor whose Spartan attitude was not all a facade. Like most programs of the time, "Martin Kane" was broadcast live from Manhattan, and Tracy was far from enthusiastic about the cluttered nature of live TV. "All those people standing around, the mikes and cameras moving in on you, the cables lying in wait for unwary feet take getting used to. It's a wonder we get through the shows without falling on our faces." Mark Stevens inherited the part in 1954, about whom we'll speak more in chapter 2.

A cross between Sherlock Holmes and Sam Spade, "Martin Kane" was joined in these ascending hours of evening by Ralph Bellamy as private investigator Mike Barnett, the "Man Against Crime." Unlike Tracy, Bellamy was thrilled about making the transition from motion pictures to television:

> I can see the day when television will span the world. I'm told that this day will come, not in our lifetime, but maybe in fifty years. But think of what that will mean in terms of common understanding, when we really learn how the other half lives. Then we may at last achieve peace.

For the present, however, Bellamy had reservations about TV of an entirely different sort, opinions by no means unique to the time. "We need writers," he complained to a reporter, "not radio writers, nor movie nor stage dramatists. Television writers, who think only in terms of its limitations and potentialities." When men like Rod Serling and Stirling Silliphant came to television in the early fifties, they brought with them the seeds of such tailored-for-television material.[5]

Barnett was less stoic than Kane and, although he didn't carry a gun, was big on slugfests. Indeed, his stamina was a marvel to *TV Digest*[6] reporter Hank O'Hare, who was moved to note in 1950: "I never cease to wonder at the pounding his skull can take, usually via blackjack." However, like his more austere counterpart, Barnett would not indulge in even a hint of romancing. The producers didn't want any soft spots in their hero's shield. Even vanity was far from the minds of these dedicated lawmen, whose standard attire was the fedora or wide-brim skinner and a trench coat. This was an atmospheric holdover from the film detective who spent most of his crime-busting hours slinking about muggy piers, trudging through misty moors, or haunting rain-soaked side streets. Actually, it was also a fiscal consideration. Since the word in early television was *economy*, a wardrobe consisting of a single trench coat was a budgetary as well as aesthetic plus.

Unfortunately, finances did not increase proportionately with the number of action and adventure programs

One of the earliest detective shows, about which very little is known, was "Barney Blake, Police Reporter." It was apparently seen only in the East and starred, from left to right, Judy Parrish, Gene O'Donnell, and Joan Arliss. O'Donnell played Blake, and Miss Parrish was his girl friend, Jennifer Allen.

Kirk Alyn as the serial "Superman."

that reached the home screen the following season. Five such shows came to television in 1950, the most enduring of which was "Superman." Like "Hopalong Cassidy" and "The Lone Ranger," "Superman" was filmed in Hollywood. It ran for seven seasons and featured George Reeves as the Man of Steel. "Superman's" twelve-year trip to television touched every conceivable intermediary base. Created by writer Jerry Siegel and artist Joe Schuster, the character premiered in the first issue of *Action Comics* (June 1938). The following year Superman got his own comic book *and* a daily newspaper strip. A radio program made its debut in 1940, seventeen short, full-color "Superman" cartoons were produced by Paramount Pictures and Max Fleischer ("Popeye," "Betty Boop") between 1941 and 1943, and George Lowther's novel, *Superman*, was published by Random House in 1942. Athletic screen star Kirk Alyn portrayed the Man of Steel in a pair of serials, *Superman* (1948) and *Atom Man vs. Superman* (1950), and George Reeves assumed the role in one feature film, *Superman and the Mole Men* (1952), released during the program's second season. The

George Reeves as Superman, with Phyllis Coates (second from right) as Lois Lane. Note the haphazard fit of Reeves' costume around the waist as opposed to that of Kirk Alyn.

theatrical films *Superman and the Jungle Devil* (1953) and *Superman Flies Again* (1954) were full-length productions edited from several episodes of the TV series.[7]

Superman was born on the planet Krypton, a world whose red sun gave it greater gravity than our yellow sun gives the earth. Thus, when Krypton exploded and the baby Kal-el's father sent him to our world in a rocket, the youngster grew up with powers that were, according to the show's introduction, "far beyond those of mortal men." Superman maintained the alter ego of Clark Kent, "a mild-mannered reporter for a great metropolitan newspaper," a disguise that permitted him to move freely among earth people, while his job with the tabloid allowed Kent to keep on top of situations that might require Superman's attention. On the surface, then, it would appear that there can be no greater hero than the amazing man from Krypton. But this determination

depends upon our interpretation of the term *hero*. Thus far, we have used it in a rather broad sense—to describe a person who works to achieve justice. But there is a side to the heroic identity that goes deeper than simple deed. If we judge Superman solely by Bowra's idea that the hero is defined by the degree of his powers, then he is indeed the zenith of heroism. His supreme energies were always applied to the good, and he was never bested. However, the elements of danger and challenge were missing in the "Superman" series, where his foes were generally two-bit hoodlums. These circumstances were dictated by a budget that could not afford the exotic monsters, disasters, and alien civilizations of Superman's comic-book or cartoon adventures. Hence, to create interest in the form of a threat, the screenwriters inevitably had thugs kidnap Kent's co-workers, Lois Lane and Jimmy Olsen, which required Superman to come to their rescue. Only rarely was the Man of Steel himself endangered. The show's budget notwithstanding, this was due to the fact that *Superman* had only one weakness—kryptonite, irradiated fragments of his home planet. The underworld was able to get a chunk of the rock on occasion and lured Superman into a number of traps. Perhaps the most elaborate of these was when Superman was sent to a well where they had bound Lois and was subsequently bombarded with a kryptonite ray gun from above. Levitating Lois via magic, Superman was able to use her body as a shield from the deadly rain. Which brings us to an interesting question: Since Kryptonite incapacitates Superman to the point where someone else has to rescue him, would he have willingly placed himself in danger, the way the Lone Ranger braved vollies of gun fire to aide a beleaguered sole, or Capt. Video piloted his craft through meteor showers to capture a dangerous foe? The answer is no. In cases where kryptonite was present, and someone was in danger, Superman wouldn't enter the room until the radioactive substance was removed. This is the mark of a diplomat, not a hero. Thus, Superman was a hero by

circumstance, rather than through an inherent desire to do good, or through an innate nobility of character. Would he have become a crime-fighter on Krypton? Probably not. Certainly Ranger Reid would have, or even Martin Kane. Superman's strength, then, made him a formidable adversary but did not automatically place him in the fore of the heroic ranks.

Wearing the padded-with-muscle costume of Superman was George Reeves, for whom this role was his last and most disappointing. The Iowa-born actor had made a considerable impression on the moviegoing public with his first co-starring role—that of one of the Tarleton twins in *Gone With the Wind* (1939). Unfortunately, he was called to fight in World War II and returned to find his career shattered. Reeves managed to land a few supporting roles in major films like *Samson and Delilah* (1949) and starred in a poor serial called *The Adventures of Sir Galahad* (1949) before donning the red, yellow,

George Reeves and Phyllis Coates in TV's "Superman."

Another sparsely documented hero is Commando Cody, who was seen over NBC for a half-hour on Saturday mornings. Judd Holdren played Cody, the Sky Marshal of the Universe; Aline Towne was his friend Joan.

and blue costume of Superman. After several seasons as the Man of Steel, Reeves started to look for acting jobs that offered more creative challenge. He was told that the public would accept him only as Superman. Frustrated and in need of money, the actor hired himself out as a professional wrestler, and was able to get a few bookings. Then, on 16 June 1959, his fiancée Lenore Lemmon—whom he was to marry within the week—and writer Robert Condon came to spend the night at Reeves' exclusive Benedict Canyon home above Beverly Hills. They all went to bed around midnight but were awakened at 2:30 A.M. by the arrival of mutual friends Carol Van Ronkel and William Bliss. Reeves argued with Bliss about the lateness of the hour but quickly apologized for his outburst. He excused himself, explaining that he was tired. When he was gone, the thirty-five-year-old Lenore looked at Condon and said, "He's going to shoot himself." The writer laughed, but the woman continued. "He's opening a drawer to get the gun." Just then, a shot echoed through the house. "See! I told you!" Lenore screamed. The guests ran upstairs to Reeves' bedroom and found him lying naked on his bed, shot once through the temple with a bullet fired from a Luger. There was no suicide note. Lemmon later said that he killed himself because, ironically, "he was known as Superman to nine million children, but couldn't get a job."

Like Reeves and William Boyd, star Gene Autry and his sidekick Pat Buttram sought to buffer their income from the dwindling movie market of 1950 by taking to the wide-open spaces of television. And, like Boyd, the Singing Cowboy and star of dozens of films and serials made between 1935 and 1953 also produced his own series, filmed in Hollywood under the banner of Flying A Productions. Indeed, so successful was the modern-day action format of "The Gene Autry Show" that it led to a spin-off series featuring Autry's steed and called "Champion: The Wonder Horse." This was followed, in 1952, by a Flying A series entitled "Range Rider," a show more violent than Autry's own. In fact, so strongly identified was "Range Rider" with rock 'em sock 'em histrionics that star Jock Mahoney and co-star Dick West took a ten-minute stunt-fight display on the rodeo circuit, where they were a top draw. In answer to critics, however, Mahoney didn't feel that violence affected a child's attitude toward the character one way or the other. He felt they were moved by ideals and not the ways in which they were manifest.

> Psychologically, children are looking for and should have security. If they can find a hero that they can put their trust and faith in, they will try to emulate said hero and live up to his teachings, by their actions and dealing with their playmates and their parents.

Autry himself was easily the nattiest cowboy in the West, owning a wardrobe of over three hundred embroidered, braided, and sequined costumes.[8] And

Frankie Thomas as "Tom Corbett: Space Cadet."

24

Gene Autry and Pat Buttram.

while younger viewers wished for less guitar-strumming and more hard riding on the range, Autry straddled the fence admirably, painting a romanticized portrait of the West while providing something for every taste. He was certainly not a "tough" hero in the tradition of the Lone Ranger but was principled, stalwart, and fought well when he had to. Among his escapades included such stories as "The Sheriff of Santa Rosa," with Autry helping the law to capture a gang of horse thieves, and "TNT," the fitting nickname for a rancher's rambunctious eleven-year-old daughter.[9]

Meanwhile, the success of "Capt. Video" as both an entertainment and merchandising property inspired the creation of "Tom Corbett: Space Cadet," a quarter-hour series broadcast every other afternoon. A year later, in 1951, the science-fiction entry was moved to a Saturday night, half-hour berth, replacing Victor Borge's variety show. Corbett and select members of the Space Academy were the featured players in this series, heroes who went flitting about the solar system of 2322 onboard their rocket ship *Polaris*. Youthful star Frankie Thomas came to the lead role with over four thousand radio programs to his credit, as well as featured parts in such films as *Boys Town* (1938) and *The Major and the Minor* (1942). His superior, the stern Commander Arkwright, was played by the stern Carter Blake. Al Markin portrayed Cadet Astro, Margaret Garland was Dr. Dale, and Jo Spence was Norma Clarke, the first woman cadet.

Like the supporting characters, Corbett was a two-dimensional hero of the serial school, serviceable as an even-handed pawn to further the series action. However, his lack of depth didn't bother the program's millions of fans nor Thomas himself, who expressed his affinity for the show in terms that were not at all atypical for the time: "I'm just thankful for living in a country where minds are free to dream of a future in which the cooperation of nations has brought about an earth united in peace." It is interesting to note that to Thomas, Al Hodge, and William Boyd, the spiritual basis of their work was of greater importance than its artistic merit. But while this may have been enough to keep the kiddies content, adults—no doubt the same people who were afraid that television was corrupting their children—wanted programming of a more cathartic nature, in the "Man Against Crime" vein. Thus, the networks came up with "Ellery Queen," "I Cover Times Square," "Big Town," and "Rocky King: Private Eye," for after-dinner broadcast in the 1950 season.

"Rocky King" was the finest of these series, starring the talented Roscoe Karns as the clever and soft-spoken big city chief inspector. Instead of violence and action, the program showcased the character himself, a detective who was human and believable. This was exactly what the veteran of "light comic" parts in one hundred and fifty motion pictures was after. "I met a number of detectives when I was doing *Front Page* on the stage," Karns said during the program's second season, "and I try to pattern the role after them." The actor was annoyed that his fellow TV sleuths solved cases with relative ease. Their rehearsed "brilliance" in uncovering clues or culprits tended to make the careful and methodical ways of *real* investigators seem slow and incompetent by comparison. "The cops I've met *like* "Rocky King" because the show doesn't ridicule them," Karns observed. As a hero, this character was also a favorite of the armchair detective because he was credible and, thus, identifiable. Watching "Rocky King" after a hard day's work, the viewer suffered right along with the inspector's triumphs and defeats. The audience was saying "I'm tired. Involve me in *your* problems," which is precisely what the investigator did. The fact that Rocky always solved his cases despite human failings made him all the more admirable. Remember, the challenge and odds against success are as much a part of the heroic image as is his prowess.

Another aspect of "Rocky King" that the public enjoyed was the way the program portrayed Rocky's wife Mable and his son Junior. The two were never shown on screen, which allowed viewers to embellish the sleuth's private world with whatever faces they wished. It also kept people tuning in, week after week, hoping one day to catch a glimpse of the mysterious Kings. "It gives people a guessing contest as to what they look like," Karns summed it up.

Ellery Queen, the Lee and Dannay character who was listed as both the author and protagonist of his novels, was 1950's other private eye. Lee Bowman, the star of such films as *Cover Girl* (1944), portrayed the dogged Mr. Queen, a year later handing the role to Hugh Marlowe. There was nothing extraordinary here, the "mob of suspects" formula providing a weekly diversion, but nothing more. For this reason, the public was considerably more taken with a trio of newspaper investigators in "Big Town" and "I Cover Times Square." Both programs followed the lives of big-city newspapermen, but only the gritty "Big Town," a radio mainstay for over a decade, had enduring impact. Pat McVey starred as Steve Wilson, champion of justice and star reporter for *The Illustrated Press*. Jane Nigh portrayed reporter Lorelei Kilbourne. Together, the journalists investigated affairs of public interest—such as fixed sports events, graft in the construction industry, corruption in politics, and so forth. Even more unusual, however, was the fact that "Big Town" itself would make news some three years hence, an event we'll discuss in chapter 2.[10]

The viewing audience responded favorably to these growingly sophisticated night-time series, and the upcoming years saw a staggering boom in showcases for the adult hero. And while genres remained pretty much the same, the hero did not. He evolved from the transplanted serial star to a mature character who had to accomodate the viewers tuning in after they had put Capt. Video and his brood safely to bed. Thus, if what we have just witnessed is the dawn, then what follows can safely be called the light. And, oddly enough, it is a day that has *yet* to see darkness.

2
The Hero Grows Up

I'd been offered a couple of routine private eye roles, but this thing had the ring of integrity. It tells the story of a guy who actually accomplished something.
—*Richard Carlson,*
Star of "I Led Three Lives"

The most astonishing success story of the decade would be that of the Jack Webb production "Dragnet." "Dragnet," which arrived in 1952, followed the travails of Sgt. Joe Friday (Webb) and Det. Frank Smith (Ben Alexander), both of whom belonged to the Los Angeles Police Department. Tightly written, well-acted, and based on actual records in the city's criminal files, the show rose quickly to and held the top spot on the ratings list, building to a steady audience of 38,000,000 weekly. Network reruns, under the title of *Badge 714*, occupied the fourteenth position on national popularity charts, even while its parent series was presenting first-run episodes. However, "Dragnet" is still a year away. Before we look at the considerable impact it had on prime-time television, let's look at a few of the unchanged formats.

Two programs that would become television institutions made their debut in 1951—"Roy Rogers" and "The Cisco Kid." Rogers came to TV from the movies. He was born Leonard Slye of Duck Run, Ohio, in 1912, and calling himself Dick Weston he began his career as a singer. After learning to ride and shoot, he was able to get bit parts in Gene Autry movies, which were followed

by the lead in *Under Western Skies* (1938). Like Autry, Rogers went slugging, riding, and singing his way through low-budget Westerns and struck a popular balance between myth and the caballero of reality. Gradually, action was forced to meet the lavish musical production numbers halfway, thus satiating the appetite of a large share of the moviegoing public. Now, parents as well as their children found individual pleasures in the colorful, tuneful Western yarns. The TV series, however, was all action aimed at the kiddie market. This was done not so much to earn huge ratings but to inspire youngsters to want to be like their hero, join the 1,750,000 member-strong Roy Rogers Fan Club, and rush right out to buy Roy Rogers clothes, guns, boots, spurs, hats, dolls, magazines, books, records, and so forth. Pursuant to this, Rogers painted a flawless portrait of himself. He didn't publish a standard for heroism and right behavior the way Autry did—specifically, his Ten Commandments of the Cowboy, which stressed justice, honesty, patriotism, chivalry, and a healthy respect for adults and animals—but he was a devout Christian and believed that "we owe it to the kids to lead homely, wholesome lives" both onscreen and off. This direct encouragement of clean-living, when presented in the context of such harmless adventures as "Go For Your Gun" and "Desert Fury," made the television Rogers a grand, if one-dimensional hero. Of course, as one might have suspected, there grew to be a great rivalry for the title of King of the Cowboys between Rogers and Autry. This "feud" was a holdover from the movie days, but it

Dale Evans and Roy Rogers.

never bothered Rogers. "He has his following, and we have ours" he noted. "There's plenty of room on the prairie." Rogers went on to say that their respective popularity "takes a relationship, a bond between the star and his audience which has nothing to do with this week's script." Contrarily, the Cisco Kid had his field all to himself. A bit of a rogue, he was a welcome contrast to the singing cowboys who, no matter what the action or circumstance, never got their fancy and hardly functional clothing dirty.[11]

The star of "The Cisco Kid" was forty-seven-year-old Duncan Renaldo, who hailed from Camden, New Jersey, but who had been raised in Versailles, France. He had had a successful cinema career before moving to television, having costarred in such prestigious films as *Trader Horn* (1930), *For Whom the Bell Tolls* (1943), and *Bridge at San Luis Rey* (1944). As for the Cisco Kid, the character himself had been featured in a number of films but never enjoyed one continuing star or interpretation. Thus, Renaldo was free to create his own very free-wheeling characterization, with the consideration the "The Cisco Kid" was aired in early prime time—from seven o'clock to seven-thirty in most parts of the country. This meant that the show had to appeal to both an adult and juvenile audience. It was a ticklish trim to achieve. Renaldo did not want to portray the inherently broad-humored swashbuckler of the West with tongue thrust so irrevocably in cheek that it couldn't be removed. Nor did he want Cisco to be a gun-slinging avenger like the Lone Ranger. Thus, the happy medium was a man who liked to talk to his horse Diablo, joke with his sidekick Pancho (Lee Cardillo)—who loved food and sleep above all else, and rode a mount appropriately called Loco—and flirt with women. Cisco was generally an amiable fellow, unless provoked by a gross injustice. No less a man of heroic deed than the Lone Ranger or Hopalong Cassidy, the Cisco Kid was simply not as deathly serious about the world as were his contemporaries.

Like the Western, science fiction for youngsters was well represented in two new entries—"Flash Gordon" and "Space Patrol." Based on the newspaper comic strip, "Flash Gordon" presented chapters from three fifteen-part serials starring Buster Crabbe, along with new adventures featuring Steve Holland. Unfortunately, the new material lacked the flair and imagination of the serial presentation, making it an awkward and poorly received package. "Space Patrol" was a more ambitious and popular effort, being the adventures of Commander Buzz Corry (Ed Kemmerer), right-hand man to the Security Chief of the Universe, Major Robertson (Ken Mayer). Lyn Osborn portrayed Cadet Happy, a character

Duncan Renaldo as the Cisco Kid.

Ed Kemmer (left) and Lyn Osborn of "Space Patrol."

29

Buster Crabbe as Flash Gordon.

who was the same age as most of the viewers, thus effecting an important camaraderie. In addition to fighting intergalactic peril from on board their spaceship *Terra IV*—a set built at the cost of $30,000—the members of the Space Patrol introduced some very popular colloquialisms to the English language, which kids enjoyed using in daily conversation; for example: "He's lost his rockets" was futuristic slang for "He's lost his mind"; "Smokin' Rockets!" was a mild oath akin to "Blazes!"; "Blast off!" meant "Get lost." While this dialogue caused English teachers to suffer many sleepless nights, parents loved "Space Patrol" simply because no one was ever killed on the show. Paralyzer rays were used to put antagonists into suspended animation, whereupon scientists would pluck the evil from their brains and make them productive members of society.

Meanwhile, the police and detective ranks swelled considerably during the year, with twelve shows scrapping for an audience. And they weren't only fighting one another! Groucho Marx's popular "You Bet Your Life" was entering its second season; "I Love Lucy" had just premiered; Sid Caesar's hilarious and legendary Your Show of Shows was beginning its third network go-around; and talent like Jack Benny, Jackie Gleason, Eddie Cantor, Bob Hope, Frank Sinatra, and George Burns were given their own programs. So the competition was formidable, to say the least. Yet, when the dust settled, the dicks had fared better than Cantor and Sinatra, although there were exceptions.

"Radio Patrol" was a short-lived, fifteen-minute-long, daily afternoon program that was too brief to hook the serious viewer, and too routine to attract the fans of "Tom Corbett" or "Hopalong Cassidy." Likewise, Dick Tracy made an unsuccessful jump from the comic's page to the home screen, with Ralph Byrd cast as the Chester Gould character who was celebrating his twentieth anniversary. However, this series' failure was not due to poor production values or a lack of followers. In four movie serials produced between 1937 and 1941, Byrd had made the square-jawed hero his own. So he was at home on television, facing an elaborate crop of Gould villains, including the immortal Flattop, the Mole, Breathless Mahoney, and many others. Unfortunately, on 18 August 1952, before filming could get underway for a second season, Ralph Byrd died of a heart attack. He was forty-three years old. Elsewhere, "Charlie Wild: Private Detective," starring John McQuade, and "Front Page Detective," with fifty-nine-year-old Edmund Lowe as reporter Dave Chase, also began brief runs, while "Racket Squad," "Treasury Men in Action," "Mr.

CBS called "Out There," which premiered in 1951, "a science series which, through special effects and trick photography, 'penetrates' the regions beyond the earth." On the left is Wesley Addy as Commander Xeglon of an alien space patrol; on the right is Robert Webber as Capt. Bill Hurley, a U.S. rocket flyer. This, according to the original caption, "is a dramatic encounter after the patrol craft captures the American and his rocket ship." Note Andy's sneakers and Webber's whistle.

Ralph Byrd as Dick Tracy.

District Attorney," "Crime Photographer," "Homicide Squad," "Foreign Assignment"—later called "Foreign Intrigue"—and "The Plainclothesman" each dug in for several seasons on the air.

"Mr. District Attorney" was presented biweekly, alternating with and quickly eclipsing "The Amazing Mr. Malone," starring Lee Tracy as a criminal lawyer. Author-actor-producer Phillips H. Lord's creation moved to television from a twelve-year tenure on radio, carrying actor Jay Jostyn with it. Possessing a marvelously authoritative voice, Jostyn used it to compensate for his lack of physical presence. He also had fine support in Len Doyle as his deputy Harrington, and Vicki Vola as Miss Miller, his secretary. Most important, however, was that the plots themselves were of a more relevant nature than most programs at this time, even dealing with such problems as drugs in high school for the famous "Case of the Bindle Boy" episode. This orientation not only made the series unique but made Jostyn a different kind of hero. While his was a battleground of wits and violence on occasion, he was also a man who used psychology and compassion when they were called for. TV justice is often black and white: the Lone Ranger, for example, was good; Butch Cavendish was bad. But Jostyn's humanitarianism suggested boundaries that were not as clearly defined. In essence, "Mr. District Attorney" was the closest that television had come to emulating a hero who was more than skin-deep. Unfortunately, it was not an example well taken.

"Treasury Men in Action" had all the earmarks of being an engrossing and mature program, but it was ultimately marred by interference from the United States Treasury Department. The series was based on actual agency cases but reduced to the formula of crime, slipup, fight, and capture. Basically, everyone's creative energies were spent in praising the government operatives, rather than producing interesting stories, which was really the fault of the department. The only freedom they gave series scripters was with the dialogue of smugglers, counterfeiters, moonshiners, and so forth. The agents had to speak perfect English—"Yes" instead of "Yeah," for instance—and their personalities had to be strictly regimented. The Treasury Men could never refer to something as having been *my* job or responsibility; it was always the *department's* effort. Not surprisingly, in terms of characterization, the agents were also of pristinely flawless stock. Their guns remained holstered unless our heroes were fired upon, and the government insisted that the men playing agents not so much as ruin the crease in their pants during an altercation. Thus, as

John Hoyt (left) and Jed Adler of "Treasury Men in Action."

one might imagine, the actors themselves were solid citizens, especially fifty-seven-year-old Walter Greaza, who portrayed the Chief. Of him, producer Everett Rosenthal said, "I'm sure Walter could walk through customs at the New York Docks easily. All hands would probably greet him as 'chief'!"[12]

Obviously, a show like "Treasury Men in Action" pushes the concept of heroism and incorruptibility to an absurd level. There is a fine line between the hero and the demigod, and the Treasury Men zigzagged indiscriminately across that border. And what they created were neither heroes or men but unrounded figures buried beneath the trappings of heroism. On the other hand, "Racket Squad" was less a myth than an overdramatization. The specialty of the so-called "bunco" squad was just that—to debunk frauds and con men and root out swindlers. Reed Hadley starred as Capt. Braddock, a cool and just operator who fell prey to stories that were laden with stifling melodrama. The victims of a raw deal were always caricatures, reacting with excessive depression or anger, which paved the way for the stabilizing influence of Braddock. Among his more renowned cases were "Desperate Money," wherein a businessman was caught in the jaws of a loanshark, and "Romance

Market," about a soldier who had been duped by a "friendship club." Unfortunately, the result of these sensationalized plots and players was that they made the Captain and his men seem lackluster by comparison. Obviously, this is not the ideal persona for a hero to project. While low-keyed bravery may get the job done, the public has always preferred heroes with hubris. They're the ones who become legend while their peers remain simply history! For instance, the impulsive Darren McGavin was photojournalist Casey in the radio-originated "Crime Photographer." His territory was more the unscrupulous lawyer or accountant than underworld killers and thieves. But he was more than just a dauntless force of justice; he had gumption, and wore it on his sleeve. "Foreign Assignment" also had flair, as newspaperman and international troubleshooter Robert Cannon (Jerome Thor) traveled around the world fighting Fascists on the Scandinavian Peninsula, searching for a faulty container of isotopes, rescuing a hunted Polish scientist, and so forth. Michael Powers (James Daly) replaced Cannon during the 1954 season, and Christopher Storm (Gerald Mohr) succeeded him a year later. By this time, however, the concept had been altered: Storm owned a casino hotel in Europe, on whose doorstep fate was always dropping dangerous packages.

To quote the original caption: "James Daly, star of Foreign Intrigue, *is busy at work filming on location in Europe. Already one of television's top dramatic actors and winner of the Daniel Blum Theatre Award, Daly is at work under the expert tutelage of* Foreign Intrigue's *producer Sheldon Reynolds (right)."*

Sometimes intelligence agents would die just outside the establishment, entrusting Storm with international secrets; at other times, people were shot during card games or in suites, and it was the host's job to find out why. Whichever the season, however, "Foreign Assignment" had continental polish that was a welcome television first. Flavoring this mixture of suave characterization and standard violence was the fact that the series was filmed entirely in Europe.[13]

The remaining law versus crime entries of 1951 were "Homicide Squad" and "The Plainclothesman." "Homicide Squad" was a routine affair starring Tom Conway as detective Mark Saber. Saber's beat was murder, but as situations became redundant he branched into less-heinous crimes. Conway and his brother, George Sanders, had both played the debonair Michael Arlen character The Falcon in the movies, and it proved a viable training ground. The Falcon, who was given his own television series in 1954, was a sleuth remarkably like Saber. Both were polished in manner, but Saber was also a man with a mind. So the bow-tied Conway always approached a case cerebrally—*alluding* to the assistance of police and lab boys, although their work was never shown. This gave the desired impression that Saber was an omnipotent crime-fighter, something that rankled the sensibilities of real detectives but created a strong central figure. Another element that made "Homicide Squad" an engrossing entertainment was the fact that it allowed the viewer to solve cases along with Saber, as he eliminated suspects one by one. On hand to help the classy sleuth was Frank Burke as Sgt. Tim Maloney, an admittedly objectionable stereotype of the bumbling police officer. However, displaying rare generosity, television did not limit the police department to only one flavor of hemlock. They also created a series entitled "The Plainclothesman," a show that pulled unsolved cases from department files, re-created the crime, and then had Ken Lynch, Eloise McElhone, and Jack Orrison try to find out whodunit. Thus did the young medium add pretention to insult and injury!

Meanwhile, it was almost all quiet on the Western front as only one new cowboy saga made its bow in 1951. In "The Adventures of Kit Carson," the featured series on "Frontier Playhouse," Bill Williams played the legendary nineteenth-century frontiersman who, with the aide of El Toro (Don Diamond) and his trusty six-shooters, helped to tame the West. It was diversion of "The Long Ranger" school, but without the color of the brawny Masked Man.

As we mentioned earlier, "Dragnet" was the show to beat in 1952. Producer Jack Webb hit upon the idea for

Jack Webb.

"Dragnet" while playing a police lieutenant in the movie *He Walked by Night* (1948). Technical advisor on the film was Sgt. Marty Wynn of the Los Angeles Police Department, and Webb asked him about the possibility of doing a radio series based on actual case histories from the department's past. Wynn routed Webb through the proper police channels, and the idea of presenting policemen as hard-working and serious-minded individuals appealed to officials. Thus, the show went over the airwaves later that year. Webb portrayed Friday, and Barton Yarborough was Smith. The program's popularity inspired Webb to carry his concept of a cops 'n' robbers series for adults to television. He formed a production company, Mark VII Productions—the name has no significance other than to sound strong and prestigious—and sold the "Dragnet" idea to NBC. The series was filmed at the Walt Disney Studios, each episode budgeted at $30,000 and shot in three days. Webb worked the schedule so that the show was before the cameras for two weeks straight, after which the crew edited and scored several programs at one time.

With a project so close to his heart, it is not surprising to learn that Webb supervised every aspect of the show,

especially the scripts. If anything, it was his intention to underplay rather than overstate these dramatizations, although he always went out of his way to hammer home the theme that "crime doesn't pay." Yet, never would he allow artistic license to blur reality, or characterizations to be overshadowed by the violence that had been attendant to previous police films and television shows. His rule of thumb was "Never will there be anything in *Dragnet* that I wouldn't want my own kids to see." Indeed, Webb's quota on gunplay called for no more than one bullet to be fired every four episodes. Also unusual about Webb's organization was that the producer-star took great pains to answer each of the four hundred pieces of mail that crossed his desk every week. And if ten viewers complained about some aspect of the program, then Webb was likely to effect the change they suggested. By his reckoning, every letter represented the feelings of one hundred thousand viewers.

Not surprisingly, there were many people in Hollywood who did not like the young entrepreneur. His unique and very strong ideas about how to run the program and production company were misinterpreted, by many, as displays of ego and temperament. For example, according to Ben Alexander, who assumed the role of Smith after Yarborough had played it in the first two episodes: "Most actors don't go for Jack. They like to criticize his techniques as a director. But he's a genius." The even-tempered Smith was often called upon to mediate between the perfectionist Webb and his costars or production personnel.

It would take a season or two for the "Dragnet" imitations to roll from the production line, so there was still a fair share of unrealistic but diverting police and mystery programs in 1952. "Mr. and Mrs. North," the Frances and Richard Lockridge creations, starred Richard Denning and Barbara Britton as Jerry and Pamela North, the genre's answer to Burns and Allen. The only difference between the two was that drama had replaced the comedians' fluff. But Pamela, as Gracie Allen, was always the catalyst, the one to get the couple involved in a case, either through premeditation or accident. It would then be up to Jerry to extricate them. Along the way, of course, they would indulge in the expected wise-guy banter that oftentimes made the murder or crime seem incidental! Still in all, the characterizations were well rounded, and if the Norths were not heroes in a literal sense they were certainly fair and generous people, identifiable and fun to be with for an hour a week. Their liaison with the law was Lt. Bill Weigand, played by Francis De Sales.

Another glib character was Boston Blackie, a

reformed thief who preferred fighting crime by himself rather than with the police. Between 1941 and 1949, actor Chester Morris had played Blackie in thirteen feature films, but it was Kent Taylor who won the television role. Lois Collier portrayed his gal Friday, Mary. One of the pleasures of Taylor's character was the trepidation he caused the police, who were always unsure as to whether he was working for or against them. Blackie, of course, never did anything to encourage or allay their fears. While this is not a particularly noble trait, justice and good are always subjective. And since we saw the adventures through the eyes of Blackie, a man who had no great love for the police to begin with, this mild intimidation was in keeping with the timbre of the program. Of course, his very diluted form of antiheroism is something that will pale to insignificance beside the rebels in the sixties and seventies.

Among the efforts of 1952, in which characterization was inversely proportional to the amount of action to be had, were "Renfew of the Mounties," policing the Canadian Border; "Don Winslow of the Navy," protecting our waterways; "Dangerous Assignment," starring Brian Donlevy as the government's *public* eye—international troubleshooter Steve Mitchell; the omnibus crime programs "Gangbusters," "Assignment Manhunt," and "Crime Syndicated"; and "Biff Baker: USA," with Alan Hale and Randy Stuart as Biff and Louise Baker, private investigators involved with the import-export trade. There was even a detective show for the kiddies, as the comic-strip character Fearless Fosdick came to television in the form of Gumby-like stop-motion puppets. In fact, with the exception of "City Hospital"—the first medical show to feature a continuing doctor character (Melville Ruick as Dr. Barton Crane, whose serious demeanor set the mold for TV doctors to follow)—the remainder of the 1952 hero-oriented programs were aimed at the youngsters. "Terry and the Pirates" was another comic-strip transplant—the adventures of a young man and his Chinese valet in the Orient. John Baer was the rugged, two-fisted Terry, while William Tracy portrayed Hot-Shot Charlie. Jon Hall was the popular "Ramar of the Jungle," the white "witch doctor" Tom Reynolds, who brought science and medicine to Africa. Hall, a movie-action star, produced this series himself under the banner of Arrow Productions, shooting each episode in two days and for under $13,000. This was a pittance when one considers the "Dragnet" budget, or even the fact that $35,000 was spent on every "I Love Lucy" show. Fortunately, Hall was able to cut corners and simultaneously make his product look more expensive by using footage of Africa from old movies. Too, midway through production on the first season's programs, stock shots of animals were used. Originally, the unit had brought in lions and apes from California's Jungle Compound, but as Hall noted: "A couple of boys got pretty badly scratched up by a black panther, and when a mountain lion got loose on the set one day, that was that." However, the show was always as credible as possible. "Kids get smarter every day," Hall observed, "and you can't fool them. So we don't try to. Even our African dialogues are genuine."[14]

More sophisticated entertainment for children were the adventures of Sky King, owner of the Flying Crown Ranch. Another radio immigrant, Schyler King (Grant Kirby) and his precocious niece Penny (Gloria Winters) used an airplane in lieu of horses to patrol their southwestern holdings. While this gimmick allowed for some original plots and scenic photography, there was something about the way King *flew* into the sunset that didn't seem quite right. Certainly the airborne heroics didn't fit a Western setting the way they belonged to the world of one of television's most fondly remembered heroes, Capt. Midnight. Created by writers Robert M. Burtt and Willfred G. Moore, the good Captain (Richard

According to the original caption, "Captain Midnight (right) and his sidekick Ikky jet-plane to the rescue when they learn that foreign agents have stolen the formula to a powerful radio-active element in Murder by Radiation."

Webb) was head of the Secret Squadron—and veteran of both a radio series and a fifteen-chapter movie serial, *Capt. Midnight* (1942). Midnight, along with his sidekick, Ichabod "Ikky" Mudd (Sid Melton), used a jet plane laden with weapons of superscience to visit trouble spots the world over. In "Mark of Death," for example, the dauntless duo flew to India to put down an uprising; "The Jungle Pit" saw them travel to a Pacific Island where aggressive Japanese soldiers were unaware that World War II had ended; and "Mystery of the Forest" had the Captain and Ikky seeking the cause of strange explosions in the American Midwest. Utterly righteous and ready to battle the forces of evil at any cost, Capt. Midnight was the epitome of the fifties' television hero. For beyond his innately exciting adventures were the carefully executed trappings of a contemporary hero. Despite the magnificence of his plane and its scientific gadgets created by Midnight's associate Tut (Olan Soule), the "Capt. Midnight" adventurers were more plausible than the extraterrestrial exploits of Capt. Video or Tom Corbett. Even the jet was credible, fantastic enough to belong to tomorrow, but not so futuristic as to have been beyond the technology of 1952. Likewise, the stories were all contemporary, which gave Midnight a head start over the slightly antiquated Lone Ranger and his brood in the race for audience identification. To complete his image as the ultimate hero, Midnight wore a snappy flyer's uniform, which served as a heroic symbol the same way that a colorful costume is the trademark of a comic-book hero.

It is interesting to note that, after only four years of operation, television had already filled its rosters primarily with successful characters from other media, or adventure stories within proven genres. Thrilling though Capt. Midnight and Sky King may have been, they were still premeditated heroes, chock-full of standard characteristics and stories. However, this is not necessarily to their disadvantage. As we indicated earlier, when an innovation surfaced, such as "Dragnet," it was mimicked and quickly became just another face in the crowd. What saved "Dragnet," however, and what will distinguish other efforts as we go along—be they imitation or original—is the care with which they were made, and the degree to which they impressed the audience at which they were aimed. Aesthetics notwithstanding, it is really the element of audience appeal that determines a television hit.

Unfortunately, 1953 was a season of very few hits. There were a number of routine detective shows, like "The Hunter," starring Keith Larsen; Donald Woods in "Craig Kennedy"; "City Detective" with Rod Cameron;

and "I Am the Law," starring George Raft as Lt. Kirby. The world travelers were Doug Carter (Stacy Harris), who stepped through the "Doorway to Danger," and into international intrigue, and actor Dan Duryea, who, in "The Affairs of China Smith," worked for either the law or the underworld in Singapore, depending upon who could pay the most money for his services. The Western rehash was Guy Madison as "Wild Bill Hickcok," featuring Andy Devine as his jovial friend Jingles; the first "Dragnet" imitation was "Pentagon Confidential," a program based on government records, but sponsoring a "Treasury Men in Action" mentality. Science fiction was spoken for by "The Atom Squad," about a group of versatile young earthmen who tackled problems in space, and the popular "Rod Brown of the Rocket Rangers," starring Cliff Robertson as the planet-hopping hero. Incidentally, "Rod Brown" was one of the few adventure series that was still being broadcast live from New York.

An irony of innovative programming is that unique shows are either well conceived or ridiculous. There is no middle ground. Oddly enough, one would have assumed that by combining a pair of popular genres like the government agency and the Western, Hollywood would have had an unbeatable conglomerate. Unfortunately, this wasn't the case with "Cowboy G-Men." Russell Hayden and Jackie Coogan starred as Pat and Stoney, men who served the government out West during

Entitled "Marking Time in Space," this photo contained the following legend: "Rod Brown of the Rocket Rangers celebrates its first anniversary and the ever-hungry Wilbur Wormser is strictly in character when he spots the birthday cake. The partying trio are (left to right) Senior Ranger Rod Brown (Cliff Robertson), Adjutant Wormser (Jack Weston) and Sr. Ranger Frank Boyd (Bruce Hall)."

36

the tumultuous post-Civil War years. The problem here was an inequity between the twin fields. The show stumbled in its attempt to meld the concrete, disciplined bearing of a G-Man with the dusty, make-your-own-rules world of the cowboy. However, it wasn't the concept as much as the approach that failed. Eleven years later, the idea was successfully resurrected as a spoof called "The Wild, Wild West." The key was not to play it straight but with tongue-in-cheek. On the other hand, "I Led Three Lives" was a success because it was real, as film star Richard Carlson portrayed real-life FBI man Herbert Philbrick, who posed as an insurance agent in order to join and spy on the American Communist Party. Although the writers ultimately ran out of industries for the Reds to infiltrate, and the show bogged down in a cops 'n' robbers format, Carlson's ability to keep the red-white-and-blue character human gave the show an aura of quality and believability. Needless to say, television's only Communist hunter—discounting Senator McCarthy—was an immediate success with the public. Philbrick fought for liberty in terms that were immediate to every American, and thus became a hero to both young and old alike.

Turning to the 1954 season we find two short-lived wrinkles in the prime time lineup: "John Acton," starring Harry Holcombe, was an early version of "The Waltons," as an Irish-American family struggled to survive in the Ohio Valley of the 1920s; while "Operation Neptune" was the story of Commander Hollister (Tod Griffin) and a submarine crew in the waters of the Pacific. These series played host to the extremes of sophistication and puerility, respectively, with the result that they both died. However, 1954 did provide an interesting display of fireworks in the person of a film-star-come-to-television. In the wake of "Dragnet's" popularity, police efforts underwent immediate changes. And one show that had it's face lifted drastically was "Martin Kane," which was given its fourth television interpretation by the youthful and rugged Mark Stevens. The strong-willed Stevens came right in and made changes. He did away with Kane's pipe trademark, having him smoke cigarettes instead. Stevens felt that butts were less pretentious and were generally associated with a younger man, one to whom the audience could relate. The show's cigarette sponsor was not about to argue. The actor also went through the scripts and knocked out every reference to Martin as Marty. "It's a corny name," Stevens decided, "and not masculine enough." In essence, Stevens wanted an absolutely authentic show. The veteran of such starkly realistic films as *The Snake Pit* (1948), *Street with no*

Name (1948), and sixteen other pictures, Stevens told an interviewer:

We avoid phoniness. Detectives like Kane are hard workers; pluggers, not master-minds and wise guys. The legendary private eye is a myth, sometimes a laughable one. That business about the slick "eye" solving the cases himself, then handing over the crooks, wrapped in cellophane paper to the dim-witted police, is nonsense. Another fallacy is unnecessary violence. If I can possibly avoid a brawl being written into the script, I'll ask for it to be eliminated.

However, an example of the realism for which Stevens was pushing leaves more than a little to be desired. In one episode, for instance, his clues to a killer's identity were that his name was Tom, he wore an 11A shoe, and he liked to shred paper when he doodled! Compare this to a contemporary "Dragnet" story wherein a druggist was beaten, robbed, and told that he and his family would be killed if he called the police. One must also wonder what right a star has to demand that changes be made in a series, rather than to suggest and discuss these alterations with his costars and directors. This, however, is an argument for another time.

Regardless of their maturity, the other new shows of 1954 also strove for a sense of pseudorealism. "Justice" was one such program, a sincere and engrossing effort and the first of what would be many "lawyer" shows in television's future. The distinguished Gary Merrill portrayed a Legal Aide Society attorney, who plied his trade in defense of the impoverished and downtrodden. The first television program to deal honestly with the problems facing poor people, "Justice" was well done and hard-hitting. In fact, so convincing were the efforts of actor Merrill that many people requesting help from the organization asked for him to handle their case. Regretfully, not everyone was taken with the show's depressing candor, and its run was brief. More successful was "Big Story," an anthology series that presented each week the true story of a courageous reporter who nailed down a feature in the face of natural disaster, the underworld, the government, big business, and so forth. To enhance viewer identification, the cases were not limited to papers of *The New York Times* stature: among the featured reporters were Wallace B. McCollum of *The New Mexico Tribune*, Robert Cour of the *Denver Post*, and other more or less "just plain folk" journalists.

This move toward the authenticity of "Dragnet" was not, however, an absolute. There were series quite willing to adopt its semidocumentary format, while adding a pinch of flamboyance as well. "The Lineup" was one such program, starring Tom Tully as Inspector

Grebb and Warner Anderson as Lt. Guthrie. Cut from the same cloth as Friday and Smith, the men faced nemeses that were somewhat more colorful than the "Dragnet" hoodlums. For example, there were such characters as a masked robber who quoted Shakespeare to his victims to lead police on false trails; and a madman who escaped from a mental institution, and about whose whereabouts no one would give the police any clues. "Col. March of Scotland Yard" was on a more or less identical conceptual plane, with a marvelously underplayed lead in very bizarre settings. Boris Karloff was the one-eyed lawman, the very picture of a professional Yard operative: soft-spoken and benevolent, but with an underlying stratum of tenacious fervor for his work. And no one could have balanced the calm and the storm better than the late, great Karloff. Among March's cases were to locate an industrialist who had faked his death in order to swindle counterfeit monies from his partner, and to protect a group of scientists from a jealous explorer who had disguised himself as the Abominable Snowman, with intentions of killing the men one by one.

Meanwhile, with considerably less originality and showmanship, there was an attempt to make "Mr. District Attorney" more relevant by slipping David Brians into Jay Jostyn's shoes, to uncover protection rackets, betting syndicates, and such. However, the producers missed the boat by equating Brians' dour bearing and plots about organized crime as fire-tempered realism. Another miscue starred Reed Hadley, newly retired from "Racket Squad," as Mathews, the "Public Defender." Mathews was a government-paid lawyer who, like Gary Merrill in "Justice," helped those in need. For some reason, however, the writers viewed poverty and innocence as one and the same, a simple-minded analogy that was aggravated by an apparently disinterested Hadley. While a program can be naive and entertaining—like "The Cisco Kid"—when its naivete stems from ignorance rather than romance, the results can be atrocious.

Before we look at the less-pretentious genre efforts of 1954, attention should be called to a novel "public servant" showcase called "Alarm." Based on the naturally dramatic and always-relevant conflict of man versus fire, it was unnecessary to dress up the program's action with contrived menace and topicality. Paradoxically, this same asset was also the show's worst enemy, as there are only so many ways to write a fire story! It was a problem that the series "Firehouse" would conquer in 1974, but just barely. In any case, during "Alarm's" limited run, it presented a rounded if fictionalized view of what makes a fire fighter (Richard Arlen) tick, giving depth and humanity to a profession of which the public generally sees only its heroic manifestation.

Despite his familiarity through such shows as "Foreign Assignment" and "Dangerous Assignment," the cosmopolitan hero drew its second wind with Cesar Romero as a diplomatic courier in "Passport to Danger." Romero's sense of humor and smooth way with the ladies was certainly a new angel; and, more often than not, it was Romero's desire to help a girl, or his betrayal by a seductress, that involved him in various and covert international doings. On the other hand, the shopworn and sullen detective was also back with no new twists, as Mike Waring, alias "The Falcon" (Charles McGraw), the unseen "Whistler," "Sherlock Holmes" (starring Ronald Howard, son of Leslie, as Holmes, and H. Marion Crawford as Watson), Mike Laynard, a.k.a. "The Lone Wolf" (Louis Hayward), and "The Cases of Eddie Drake" (Don Haggarty) came to the home screen. Only "Sherlock Holmes" had anything to offer the telefan, boasting atmospheric location photography, classic stories, and good performances by all.

The remaining series featuring a heroic lead were somewhat more inventive. Of course, with twenty new shows premiering in 1954, there was bound to be some ground-breaking, as in "Waterfront," an utterly preposterous but highly enjoyable series about the tugboat *Cheryl Ann* and her stout-hearted captain, John Herrick (Preston Foster). Ordinarily, of course, tugboats spend their days escorting freighters and ocean liners to and from the open sea. But there was none of this conventional labor for the *Cheryl Ann!* She carried her crew through adventures with smugglers, saboteurs, and escaped convicts—all of this amidst the impressive backdrop of an actual San Pedro, California, harbor locale. In fact, the scenery was often given parity with the performers—something Foster didn't seem to mind: "I appear in maybe a third of the footage in each show, and in some episodes I hardly appear at all. That's all to the good. People can get sick and tired of the sight of you in a week-in, week-out basis." Regardless, *Cheryl Ann* of the "Waterfront" was a perfect example of romantic *ingenue* as escapist fare. Speaking of which, one girl on whom the label "innocent" cannot be tagged is Gail Davis, the twenty-five-year-old star of Gene Autry's popular "Annie Oakley." The 5'2" Gail came to Hollywood in 1949 and was immediately given a supporting role in *Romance of Rosy Ridge*, a Van Heflin film that also introduced Janet Leigh to the moviegoing public. Gene Autry saw the film and gave Miss Davis a part in his picture *Cow Town* (1950). The film showcased her natural athletic and performing ability, and Autry signed the girl to play the legendary nineteenth-century markswoman on television. As Autry later remarked: "There are lots of girls who can ride and shoot, and lots of girls who can act, but the girl who could do both just couldn't be found. Then this kid comes along and I didn't have any more problems." Indeed, Miss Davis was so handy with a gun that during the summer hiatus from "Annie Oakley," she joined a touring Wild West show. The climax of her performance was to ride her TV horse Target at full tilt and light six matches with a single shot from a .22 revolver. "It's really not too difficult," she said at the time, "and at eight or ten feet head-on, how can you miss?"[15] Supporting Miss Davis in the TV series were Brad Johnson as Deputy Sheriff Lofty Craig, and Jimmy Hawkins as Tagg, her eleven-year-old brother and a lure for the younger viewers. Obviously, no red-blooded American boy would have been caught dead tuning in to watch Tagg's sister! Which brings us to the significant fact that "Annie Oakley" gave us our first real television heroine. Over the years, women have been relatively scarce as the focal point of action series, and it would be beneficial for us to analyze this impropriety.

It's a pity that there has never been a serious sociological study of the female as a hero. It might give deserved recognition to such legendary figures as the German Brunhilde, Russia's Vassilissa, or the Bible's twelfth-century Deborah. Fortunately, television offers us a microcosmic world that puts the heroine in perspective. Viewers were quite willing to have women share the spotlight with men as comedians, singers, panelists on game shows, and stars in dramatic series such as "Studio One" and "Playhouse Ninety." But in adventure programs, women were seldom used as anything other than an excuse for the hero to go into action, for example, reporter Lois Lane (Noel Niell) was captured, and Superman had to save her; or Mrs. North stumbled upon a crime and called for Mr. North to help solve it. However, to say that this was chauvinistic is to simplify matters by addressing the result rather than the cause.

The great bulk of our television heroes relied on their fists to resolve a tacky situation, or were invariably slapped around by their intended quarry during the course of an adventure. Obviously, it would not have been very gallant for producers to horsewhip their women in like fashion. Even when Annie Oakley found herself in a situation where guns were useless, it was Deputy Sheriff Craig who came to her rescue. Until it became socially and aesthetically acceptable in the sixties and seventies for women like Honey West and "Police Woman" to use jiujitsu and toss antagonists head over

heels, the action heroines *had* to be few in number. Too, as we have seen, the concept of viewer identification is a strong one in programming. Networks felt, and rightly so, that the audience of the Saturday serial matinees were the same ones who curled before the tube to watch an adventure series. In other words, they were the preteenage boys. One must assume, then, that to have kept "Annie Oakley" on the air for several seasons, if the boys couldn't identify with her, they at least enjoyed her galloping escapades; that a lot of young girls who secretly dreamed of being the no-nonsense, gun-toting cowgirl were watching; and that a number of fathers tuned in to see the attractive Miss Davis in action. In any event, the fact that there was no attempt to imitate the successful "Annie Oakley" indicates that Hollywood still had its doubts about women as characters who could possess physical and mental fortitude. Or perhaps producers had too much respect for the ladies to star them in such travesties as "Treasury Men/Women in Action" or "Mr./Ms. District Attorney."

Another minority in the realm of television drama was the animal. To be sure, Gene Autry's horse Champion had his own program, and the popular steeds of the Lone Ranger and "Roy Rogers" were often called upon to save their masters' necks. But it was the appearance of *"Lassie"* and *"Rin Tin Tin"* in 1954 that warmed the hearts of animal lovers everywhere. Even more satisfying was the fact that the collie and German shepherd, respectively, were far and away more resourceful than their human costars. And both, of course, came to TV from a successful motion-picture career. In Lassie's case, she was paired with Tommy Retig, Jan Clayton, and George Cleveland (as Gramps), who involved themselves in generally sudsy domestic situations, while Lassie saved lost dogs and children or worked out solutions to everyone's problems. Rin Tin Tin, on the other hand, had to contend with a more virile environment, aiding the steadfast Lt. Rip Masters (James Brown), his right-hand man, Sgt. Majors (Joe Sawyer), and their young ward, Rusty (Lee Aaker)— discovered with the dog after an Indian massacre—all of Fort Apache. Powerful, uncorruptible, fleet-of-foot, and always ready to act with the best interests of their owners in mind, these dogs and the other television animals represent ideal heroes!

There were few critics who did not agree that the two canines were far and away more expressive than "Medic" star Richard Boone. Boone portrayed Konrad Styner, the dour main character in one-third of the series' hard-hitting, true-to-life dramas. The show was originally a one-shot program produced by "Dragnet" cocreator

James Moser and aired as "Doctor" over the NBC radio network in 1951. "Medic" did away with the historical radio and film thesis that every patient under the featured physician's care must survive. If it weren't so in real life, then it didn't appear on "Medic." Unfortunately, where health was concerned, the public has traditionally wanted happy endings, and although "Medic" ran for several seasons, it did not enjoy the runaway success of later doctor shows. Yet, let it not be said that the televiewing public will only or automatically buy easily digested pap: "Joe Palooka," based on the comic strip, and an utterly simple-minded series, failed miserably on the tube. Palooka, of course, is the boxer who never loses a fight. Made flesh-and-blood by Joe Kirkwood, the man who played him in the movies, the pugilist knew nothing about the gambling, fixes, or temptresses that surrounded him; one merely pointed Joe in the right direction, and he fought. However, the baby-faced boxer did rely on the instincts of girlfriend Cathy Downs who, in the person of Ann Howe, sat in the crowd while Joe defended his title but stepped into the ring when an oppressed but upstanding soul came to the fighter for help.

Repeating our argument against "Superman," purity and invincibility in a character do not themselves a hero make. Richard Boone's surgeon was flawed, wont to lose his temper, and even made mistakes; then there was Joe Palooka, the very essence of all-American might and apple-pie innocence. Palooka was flat; Styner had depth. This is every bit as vital to the heroic image as his ability to act selflessly and courageously. A viewer cannot identify with a slab of granite, but he can relate to a human being. And as we enter 1955 these two kinds of heroes will be everywhere. Children will still have their "Roy Rogers" and "Capt. Midnight," ilk during the day, but prime time will be crowded with Styner-type heroes. This time, however, they will not be surgeons but cowboys, and they will dominate the airwaves for years to come. It is difficult to appreciate over twenty years after-the-fact that the so-called Adult Western almost became a genre unto itself. Very few of the villains were ornery just for the sake of being mean. Most of them sported deep-rooted neuroses, which made the frontier sheriff of the Adult Western as much a psychologist as he was a leather-slapping lawman. In chapter 3, we'll see how these revolutionary Westerns slowly infused the evening hours with tumbleweed, dust, and psychoses, displacing many of the police shows that had, thus far, reigned supreme. And in addition to this takeover, we'll see how Hollywood jumped on a bandwagon that remains unparalleled in television history.

3

The Adult Western

He went thataway—and he looked mighty manic-depressive.

—Anonymous comedian, circa 1955

Television has never suffered from a lack of adventure programs, and the midfifties were no exception. The difference between this period and any other was that the scales tipped in favor of the Adult Westerns—or, as they were called when the label became a tired one, *mature* Westerns. Before we look at these, however, let's first examine the youth fare.

Certain actors have become synonymous with the kinds of characters they play, and certainly one of the screen's consistently majestic performers was Buster Crabbe. Born in 1908, the championship athlete had portrayed such film heroes as Tarzan, Buck Rogers, and Flash Gordon, before television asked him to star as "Capt. Gallant of the Foreign Legion." Despite the locale, the typical Western plots were all in evidence, save that rustlers were now members of the secret police, bank robbers were spies, and the marshal was the Moroccan chief of police. Aiding the vigorous, duty-bound Gallant in his desert crusades were Western star Fuzzy McKnight, as an orderly, and Crabbe's real-life son, Cuffy, as a legionnaire. The first-season adventures of "Capt. Gallant" were shot in North Africa, where the climate and terrain were perfectly suited to the series. Shortly after production got underway, however, that part of the world was thrown into civil war, and the

company had to pack its cameras and leave with uncomfortable haste. They moved to a town in Italy called Tirrenia, near Pisa on the shores of the Mediterranean Sea, where bulldozers worked the beaches into dune-swept deserts, and crew members busied themselves with the care of camels imported from Arabia. For Crabbe's part, he was thrilled with the change in locale, and spent his every free moment, including entire lunch hours, swimming in the Mediterranean. Of course, while Crabbe was breast-stroking his way through water, Walt Disney was back home wending his way through the mountains of cash generated by his "Davy Crockett" television effort. Created as a three-part presentation for the weekly omnibus program "Disneyland," the legendary Western figure became the most popular hero television had ever seen. Just about every boy in the country owned a coonskin cap like the one worn by Davy; "Davy Crockett" coloring books, novels, and comic books were also popular items. The famous theme song, "The Ballad of Davy Crockett," was a top-selling record.

Crockett was brought to life by a then relatively unknown Fess Parker. The 6'5" Texan had first visited Hollywood in 1943, while in the Navy, and later said: "They took me on a tour of the lot where they were making *State Fair*, and I sort of got a hankering right there to be an actor. Looked like pretty much fun." After his discharge, Parker made nine films before landing the role of Crockett. Disney chose movie song-and-dance man Buddy Ebsen to play his fictitious sidekick, George

Fess Parker (left) and Buddy Ebsen in the "Davy Crockett" episode entitled "Davy Crockett: Indian Fighter." © Walt Disney Productions.

Russell. While the miniseries' runaway success was hardly anticipated, one can hardly say that the deck wasn't stacked in Davy's favor. It had the right combination of action, a strong, soft-spoken, and confident hero, and the Disney name—any *two* of which would ordinarily have been enough to produce a hit. Accordingly, when "Davy Crockett" clicked, the three hour-long episodes were edited into a feature-length film. Of course, the last show of the trilogy had featured the Battle of the Alamo, where Crockett, Russell, and nearly two hundred other men were killed by Mexican soldiers. This was the first time that a major hero had died in a television series, and many were the youngsters who went into mourning for the noble warrior. More important, however, is the way in which television and the profit incentive were able to conquer death! Disney was not so foolish as to let a financial giant stay long expired. *"Davy Crockett* became one of the biggest overnight hits in television history," Walt once said, "and there we were with three films and a dead hero. We tried to come back later with two more called *The Legend of Davy Crockett,* but by that time the fever had run its course. Those two never did catch on the way the original three did."

At the same time that Davy Crockett was earning his coonskin crown as the "King of the Wild Frontier," Edgar Buchanan was practicing a very subjective form of law in the short-lived series "Judge Roy Bean," while young "Buffalo Bill Jr." was busy trying to live up to his father's proud name. Actually, the two Bills were not related, although Gene Autry's Flying A Productions thought—and rightfully so—that this would be a commercial title. Bill (Dick Jones) and his sister Calamity (Nancy Gilbert) were orphans who could rope, ride, and shoot, and were adopted by one Judge Wiley (Harry Cheshire), magistrate of a small Western pioneer town. The teenage hero and heroine helped their father administer justice, and went over big with the youngsters. Less fortunate was "Brave Eagle," an intelligent and oftentimes stirring program from Roy Rogers' Frontier Productions. The show presented the vanishing West as seen from the standpoint of the Indians. The White Man was shown with neither applause or condemnation, since this was a program about the exploits of thirteen-year-old Keena Nomkenna, foster son of Brave Eagle (Keith Larsen). Each week, Brave Eagle taught his young ward a lesson about charity or justice, in a setting remarkably free of stereotypes. The Indians all spoke perfect English and were portrayed as the possessors of a great and ancient culture. Quite intentionally, this show did not boast the pace and action that was expected of a Western, which is why, before long, "Brave Eagle" had vanished from the video prairie. "Tales of the Texas Rangers" had a somewhat longer life span, as Willard Parker and Harry Lauter portrayed modern-day Rangers Clay Morgan and Jace Pearson. Riding about in police cars, our heroes were able to triumph over every evil except tremulous plotting and hollow characterizations of the sort that disappeared with the movie serial. However, not all of television's adventures for children were as routinely fashioned as "The Texas Rangers." Different genres managed to add variety to this season's juvenile entries, as "Robin Hood," "Long John Silver," and "Sgt. Preston of the Yukon" galloped, sailed, and sledded into the homes of millions.

"Robin Hood" starred former movie leading man Richard Greene as the kind-hearted thief of Sherwood Forest, who stole from the rich and gave to the oppressed subjects of King Richard. Alex Gauge played Friar Tuck, Bernadette O'Farrel was Maid Marion, and Alan Wheatley portrayed the scheming Sheriff of Nottingham. The series was shot at Nettlefield Studio in Walton-on-Thames, England, and had excellent production values, fine scripts, and a marvelous cast of characters. While

Carrying Old Betsy, his famous rifle, Davy Crockett concludes a campaign speech in "Davy Crockett Goes to Congress. © Walt Disney Productions.

adults may have found Greene's Robin Hood less vital than the fondly remembered knave of Errol Flynn, he managed to work a fair share of derring-do into the TV series. In fact, Greene himself felt that the heroic deeds and pictorial ornaments of "Robin Hood" were precisely the stuff of which legends are made:

> Kids love pagentry and costume plays, but the most important single thing is that Robin can be identified with any American hero. He's the British *Hopalong Cassidy*! For instance, one time I had to scale a high wall and shoot an arrow at the same time. I clung to the wall with one hand and pulled the bow, using my other hand, feet, and teeth, and let go.

Not content with this, Greene went so far as to repeat the old Lone Ranger trick—or gag, as screenwriters are wont to call them—of splitting a noose with an arrow, riding up to the gallows, rescuing a condemned man, and hurrying away. The fact that this kind of stunt has always been a ready part of the screen hero's repertoire does not

Willard Parker and Harry Lauter in "Tales of the Texas Rangers."

43

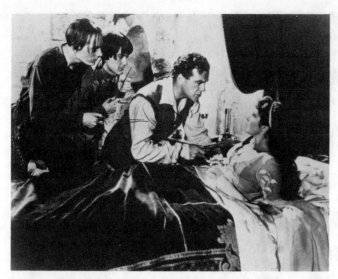

To quote CBS: "Medieval Juvenile Delinquents! Jules Michael McKeag) and Godric (Ian Whittaker) assist Robin Hood (Richard Greene) as they 'rob' Maid Marian (Bernadette O'Farell) after they have entered her mansion at midnight. Robin stages the 'robbery' to teach the two young rogues a lesson in The Intruders *episode of* Robin Hood."

Robert Louis Stevenson's scowling, quick-tempered but likeable scalawag from *Kidnapped*. Shot in Sydney, Australia, "Long John Silver" featured the immortal Robert Newton characterization of a pirate who prowled the seas of the eighteenth century. Kit Taylor portrayed his cabin boy, Young Jim Hawkins. If one can accept the premise than an affable band of cutthroats would help to defend England against Spain, then this unusual blend of comedy, action, and dubiously motivated heroics— are the pirates after booty or are they defending Her Majesty? the viewer is left to wonder—then "Long John Silver" was an enjoyable series. Less entertaining, but no less exotic, was the John Russell vehicle "Soldiers of Fortune," the story of two rough-and-ready Americans, Tim (Russell) and Toubo (Chick Chandler), who did everything from fighting rampaging elephants in India to pearl-diving in the South Seas—all in the name of adventure. There was no pretention here: the program's "motto" was action for action's sake. And, as such generally short-sighted efforts go, it was no worse than average. The same can be said for "The Count of Monte Cristo," starring George Dolenz—father of "Monkee" Mickey Dolenz—who, as a polished but bastardized

matter. Like the long touchdown pass or a favorite musical composition, it is an experience that cannot be dulled by repetition.

On this subject of redundancies, the mold from which "Sgt. Preston of the Yukon" was made is as old as recorded history itself. Whether we call the character Jason, King Arthur, or the Long Ranger, the resolute, one-dimensional hero is the root from which all other heroes spring. The brainchild of George. W. Trendle and the same staff that had created "The Long Ranger," Sgt. Preston was a less exciting but no less devoted crime-fighter than his masked counterpart. The TV version of the radio program starred superb horseman and ex-pilot Robert Simmons as the red-coated officer of the Northwest Mounted Police. Together with his faithful huskie, Yukon King, Preston lived in the doughty and strapping goldrush era, becoming involved with all the intrigue and danger confederate with mines, mountains, trappers, swindlers, and even women—as long as there was no romance. Simmons was sturdy in the title role, admitting: "This is the series I was meant for." He added, however, that it wasn't his talent as an actor that had won him the part, but the fact that he could ride. Regardless, the program was a great success and gave television its newest canine hero in Yukon King, who, like Rin Tin Tin, was often called upon to save his master in a knotty situation. In this respect, he was far more useful than the parrot that belonged to Long John Silver,

Sgt. Preston and his malemute Yukon King subdue Jack Littlefield in this publicity still for "Sgt. Preston of the Yukon."

Edmund Dante, became involved with kidnapped royalty, helped peasants to fight the wicked El Diablo, and so forth.

Apart from "Sgt. Preston," the only show to feature an animal that season was "Fury"—"The story of a horse and the boy who loved him." Actually, "Fury" was no different from "Lassie," except that there were more cinematographic long-shots so as not to crop the star. Fury was a wild black stallion captured by Jim Newton (Peter Graves), a widower and ranch owner. In town for supplies, Jim clears a young orphan named Joey (Robert Diamond) of breaking a window, and takes him home as his "son." Together with a grizzled old hand named Pete (William Fawcett), Jim, Joey, and Fury face all manner of trouble—from a forest fire to the kidnapping of Fury, to Joey's falling from the horse and lying unconscious in the mountains. Once again, no matter how brave or resourceful the humans were, the horse was the hero and he always outshined them all.

It has been said that animals are temperamental performers; that they can be cooperative one day and impossible the next. All of which goes to prove that dogs and horses are no different from people. As we leave the children's shows of 1955 behind, and turn to adult

Brian Keith and Diane Brewster of "The Crusader."

programing, we find Mark Stevens once again "raising Cain" on the set. Only this time it's not Martin Kane he's raising, but a revamped "Big Town." This was the newspaper program that, you will recall, had come to television from radio in 1951. Needless to say, the actor who had bent the "Martin Kane" format to his personal whim took excessive liberties with the existing "Big Town." He eliminated supporting players, promoted his own character, Steve Wilson, from reporter to editor, and, forming a production company, bought all rights to the show. He also took over as "Big Town's" writer, producer, and director. With these responsibilities, it is remarkable the actor retained his sanity, let alone a good or bad disposition on the set. But Stevens was not content with complete control. He wanted reality. He wanted "Dragnet." So the star pulled stories from newspaper front pages—such as the employment problems faced by men over forty, the sale of black-market blood, the low pay of school teachers, etc.—and, in so doing, exhibited an admirable sense of civic responsibility. Yet, these efforts weren't enough, and a year after the change "Big Town" was pulled from the air. Stevens slipped from creative passion to bitterness about the cancellation and offered some insights into television politics:

What happened to *Big Town* is just what happens to a lot of TV shows. The time slot the network had for it didn't justify the raising production costs, and the network wouldn't give it a better time slot because it didn't *own* the show. So the sponsor dropped it. Anyway, if "Big Town" had continued, I wouldn't have starred in it. I've decided that an actor is a pawn in a chess game, and being one no longer interests me. I'm just sick of acting.

After the death of "Big Town," and the brief runs of other detective and espionage shows mentioned earlier—as well as such efforts as "Fair Trial," "Penitentiary," and "Resistance," which never made it past the single trial episode, or *pilot*, stage—program directors deduced that the seven-year reign of the TV gumshoe and contemporary fighter for the underdog had ended. As if to emphasize this changing climate, falling swiftly before the bull were Brian Keith's "Crusader" series, about free-lance writer and champion-for-minority-causes Matt Anders; Bruce Seton as "Fabian of Scotland Yard"; and Louis Jordan as a *gendarme* in the "Paris Precinct". Broderick Crawford's "Highway Patrol," the adventures of Patrol Chief Dan Mathews, managed a longer run due to the fact that it was syndicated, meaning it was peddled to stations on an individual basis and, thus, was not subject to the decisions of network executives. But the die had been cast. TV was on the lookout for a new gimmick, and they

Hugh O'Brian faces opponent in "The Life and Legend of Wyatt Earp."

to taciturn. So I devoted seven months to reading about Earp, and I'm convinced that he was a thoroughly honest man, righteous and utterly fearless. He was also just. In two hundred gunfights, he killed only four men. He had a wonderfully subtle sense of humor, and was essentially an easy moving, relaxed type of guy. But he could tense up like a coiled spring, and he had fabulous reflexes. You stay alive through two hundred gunfights, and you've *got* to have fabulous reflexes!

Every effort was made to create sets and costumes that were accurate—down to such details as the make of Earp's gun, the Buntline Special—and for the scripts to adhere to history wherever possible. The series followed Earp from his arrival in Ellsworth City, Kansas, through his career in Dodge City, Kansas, including the famous Gunfight at the OK Corral. From the start it was a ratings blockbuster.

The second Adult Western of 1955 was "Gunsmoke," which, even more so than "Wyatt Earp," served as the prototype for this kind of program. The cornerstone of "Gunsmoke" was Matt Dillon, the introspective marshal of Dodge City.[16] Played by 6'6" James Arness, Dillon had to reason as often as fight, and he did both rather well. Faced with such problems as having to amputate a friend's leg and suffer the repercussions, or deal with a retarded youth who went on a murderous rampage, the marshal acted with sensitivity, tact, and, only as a last resort, with his gun. In short, Dillon was always ready to turn the other cheek, thus giving television its first Christian hero! Assisting Matt in his peace-keeping efforts were the game-legged deputy Chester (Dennis Weaver); the tough, strong-willed owner of the Long Branch Saloon, Kitty (Amanda Blake); and the philosopher-physician Doc Adams (Milburn Stone). Kitty, of course, was also Dillon's romantic interest. Not that the viewer was ever permitted to intrude on anything private: "The most physical contact we've had," Miss Blake observed, "is when I fainted and Matt picked me up." The reason for this platonic display was explained by Arness:

People like Westerns because they represent a time of freedom. A cowboy wasn't tied down to one place or to one woman. When he got mad, he hauled off and slugged someone. When he drank, he got good and drunk. Today, people don't have enough gumption to live the way they want to. They've grown away from their basic instincts. They're overcivilized. That is why they tune in on Western shows, to escape from conformity. And they certainly don't want to see a U.S. Marshal come home and help his wife with the dishes!

Arness may have been right, for "Gunsmoke" stayed on the air nearly twenty years. More important than

found it in the Adult Western. Only two such shows premiered that season, but ten times that number would flood the airwaves within the next two years.

"The Life and Legend of Wyatt Earp" brought a young actor by the name of Hugh O'Brian from obscurity to fame in a series based on the exploits of one of the West's most famous lawmen. O'Brian, a Marine drill instructor at eighteen, had begun his television career by working for free, at a time when the medium was young and didn't pay actors. However, O'Brian believed that television was the coming medium and wanted credentials for a time when producers could hire performers for other than experience. Naturally, when this situation came about in the late forties, O'Brian found steady employment. "You must be willing to work hard," he explained at the time, "and if you're looking for the fast buck or the lucky break, stay out of acting." As for the character who brought O'Brian his hard-earned success, he was a U.S. Marshal who lived from 1848 to 1929. Historians have mixed notions regarding Earp, about whom O'Brian said:

He's a controversial character who has been depicted as everything from saint to devil, lawman to bully, loquacious

James Arness and Amanda Blake of "Gunsmoke."

escape, however, was the fact that the series have viewers characters made of flesh and blood, who became angry and could experience sadness or joy. With few stock situations, just the right amount of action and gunplay to keep Western fans happy, and provocative scripts and performances, "Gunsmoke" became the ultimate television Western, and remains so to this day.

Contrarily, the 1956 season left a lean legacy to television history, with unusual but ultimately repetitious children's programs and Adult Westerns dominating the tube. In the latter category, it became quickly evident that the public would buy almost anything as long as it featured a taciturn hero whose personality was sketched along the Dillon-Earp lines. Accordingly, nudging the "Gunsmoke" approach to the frontier one step further from cliché, "Cheyenne" gave us the same inventive storylines and an honest, laconic hero who stood literally as tall as Matt Dillon. However, Clint Walker's Cheyenne Bodie was also a rootless man. There was no Kitty to serve as an emotional window for the

audience, with the result that Bodie was an enigma. His entire *raison d'etre* seemed to consist of lending a strong right arm to whomever might need it.

The 6'5" Walker was instantly accepted by his male audience, who wished that they had his awesome physical stature, and by women who no doubt shared this fantasy. For Walker's part, he felt that "Cheyenne" was popular simply because "people like to see a big guy like me get beat up." While this may be an oversimplification, the element of Cheyenne Bodie rising, phoenixlike, from the inevitable thrashing he took in every episode *was* a powerful aspect of his heroic identity. Within two years, however, most of the fighting on "Cheyenne" was taking place off-camera, as Walker demanded the same percentage deals—participation in the program's profits—that both Arness and O'Brian were enjoying from their shows. He also wanted to make public appearances without having to give the studio half his income. The studio disagreed, feeling that they had made him a star and were therefore entitled to the money.

Clint Walker of "Cheyenne."

Unable to come to terms, Walker left the show and the 6'2" Ty Hardin was brought in as his replacement, Bronco Layne. Helmed by the talented but ill-cast newcomer, "Cheyenne" had charted a course to Boot Hill. When the ratings fell, the producers capitulated and Walker was back in the saddle by season number three.

Meanwhile, with all these cowboys running around, it was only natural that the Adult Western give equal time to the Indian. Considering the failure of "Brave Eagle," however, Hollywood decided to go with a less-revolutionary concept. Drawing substance from the 1950 film *Broken Arrow,* a new TV series of the same name recounted the uneasy peace that existed between the Apache Chief Cochise (Michael Ansara) and the United States government, as represented by Indian Agent Tom Jeffords (John Lupton). Actually, this state of truce was selected as the series' focal point less in homage to history than because it was a means of avoiding cavalry charges and costly shootouts. Instead, there were bouts with smallpox, struggles with corrupt officials who were stealing reservation-bound supplies, and the soul-searching of Indians who found themselves torn between their heritage and the promise of the "White Eyes" world.

The final Western entry of the year was a surprisingly successful, middle-of-the-road effort starring Scott Forbes as Jim Bowie. Not a showcase for neurotic villains or controversial topics, neither was it a stage for the fairy tales so typical of the juvenile Westerns. Possessing a name laden with the weight of history's admiration, Jim Bowie might have failed as anything less than a demigod. Luckily, Forbes found a man amidst the legend and

Sir Lancelot (William Russell) captures the villainous Sir Grint (Garry Thorne) in "The Adventures of Sir Lancelot."

painted the great American hero—who died with Davy Crockett at the Alamo—as a warm and generous man, with a sense of humor and a keen eye for the ladies. He was always ready to help people in trouble, and his wanderings brought him to the aide of immigrants, fur trappers, and even such famous people as John James Audubon. These modest, people-oriented adventures helped to keep fact before myth. Even the hero's famous Bowie knife was played down, although this was due to the fear that it might appear to sanction the switchblade-carrying teenagers of the time.

There was little chance of America's troubled youth being similarly inspired by the season's other shows, especially those that were geared to young viewers. The only weapons in evidence were muskets, spears, dudgeons, cutlasses, lances, and bayonettes—instruments hardly accessible to the average teenager. Spurred by the popularity of "Robin Hood," television also gave us "The Adventures of Sir Lancelot," "Tales of the 77th Bengal Lancers," and "The Buccaneer." Similar programs planned for the 1956 season, such as "Richard the Lionhearted" and "The Three Musketeers,"—the latter featuring Jeffrey Sloane as D'Artagnon—never made it past the pilot stage.

"Sir Lancelot," made by Sapphire Films, producers of "Robin Hood" and "The Buccaneer," transposed the story of King Arthur's bravest knight from the sixth to the fourteenth century, and changed the object of his chivalry from women's carnal affections to the simple doing of good deeds. Twenty-four-year-old William Russell, the series' star and a fan of Arthurian literature said, "All our writers have done is to clean up the plots just a bit. Lancelot's loves are now strictly platonic. He is still clean-cut and never takes advantage of an opponent, although when aroused, the fellow can take on all comers." The production, scripts, photography, and acting were all top-notch—something that inspired some of the actors to emulate the characters they were playing. Russell explains:

> We had a genuine hero, of a sort. During the filming of one of the episodes, a horse stepped on David Morrell's foot. Morrell, who plays Sir Kay, couldn't dislodge the beast and was forced to stand there smiling blandly with eight hundred pounds of horse on his toes, for ten minutes of shooting.

As for the swords and other weapons, they were all real. Only the armor was faked, being made of rubber, after metal proved unworkable. "The blasted things weighed ninety pounds," Russell said, "and when they squeezed me into one, I could hardly lift the bloody axe. Then they had to hoist me into the saddle with a derrick. And whenever anyone hit me in the jousts, I went down in a lump and stayed down. Finally, they had to undress me with wrenches." Jane Hylton played Lancelot's "platonic" love Guinevere, and Robert Scroggins was the good knight's squire.

Skipping forward in time, "The 77th Bengal Lancers" were late-nineteenth-century soldiers who defended Ft. Oghora near India's famous Khyber Pass—all in the service of Queen Victoria. Phil Carey and Warren Stevens starred as sidekick lieutenants in this exciting action series. There was little expense spared to make the show authentic. Nearly $120,000 was spent to build the fort exteriors, while $50,000 was pumped into the arsenal itself: the village, soldiers' quarters, and offices. The only skimping was on the costumes; in all, only eighteen Lancer uniforms were made, and the film was carefully edited to give the appearance of several dozen soldiers in every episode. Like Sir Lancelot, the lead lieutenants of "The 77th Bengal Lancers" were upright men of courage. However, since we seldom saw the men in a noncombative situation, this is just about all we knew of them. In any half-hour's children show, it is incumbent that there be little exposition, unless it furthers the adventure element. In this respect, "The Buccaneer" was also rather shallow, as Robert Shaw's *(Jaws, The Sting)* reformed pirate Dan Tempest plied the waters of the Bahamas in 1722. His nemesis, the not-so-reformed Blackbeard (George Margo) was reminiscent of Robert Newton's "Long John Silver". The characters' innate color was reduced to fits of laughter or such strained expressions as "Well blow me down for a cross-eyed seagull"; and, unlike its companion programs, the good deeds performed in and by the Buccaneer were based less on principle than as an excuse for swordplay.

Another kiddie feature of 1956, "Sheena: Queen of the Jungle," was no more rounded than the other programs. Not a period effort like the others, although it was set in the mysterious wilds of Africa which gave it exotic allure, "Sheena" featured a character who fought to keep the jungle free from man-made impurities such as greed and wanton violence. Understanding her values, the viewer knew everything there was to know about Sheena, a female Tarzan complete with leopard-skin outfit, a pet chimp named Chim, and a counterpart for Jane—a trader named Bob (Christian Drake). She even went swinging through the trees like Edgar Rice Burroughs' ape-man. Sheena's origin was never explained, although she was clearly the self-appointed protector of the jungle. And there were few who argued with Sheena, once they met all 6'1" of her, in the person

Quoting the original CBS blurb: "Pretty Petra Davies is rescued by Robert Shaw from the clutches of Blackbeard in this scene from The Ladies *episode of* The Buccaneer. *Miss Davies, playing the role of Christine, is one of a shipload of marriageable young ladies being sent to the woman-less isle of New Providence. When Blackbeard tries to shanghai the ship and its beauteous cargo, he finds Capt. Dan Tempest (Shaw) and his men disguised in dresses already on board to frustrate his plans."*

of actress Irish McCalla. Unfortunately, Miss McCalla was about the only impressive element of the program! Shot in Mexico, the show was gleaned from the proverbial bottom of the barrel, padded with poor stock animal shots and burdened with hackneyed plots. However, Miss McCalla kept the series exciting. She did most of her own stunts, and handled a knife, spear, and bow and arrow with authority, although not without cost. "When I got back from Mexico," the actress complained, "my husband wanted to know if I'd been run over by a tank. I had spear cuts, thorn scratches, ocelot claw marks, and contusions from all the stunts I did." Inconsiderate of the technical or aesthetic aspects of the show, it is interesting to note that Sheena's sex was seldom used as a springboard for stories; for instance, none of the show's bad guys ever said anything like,

"Aw, she's only a dame." If he had, the "dame" would have served him his head on a handy frond. As far as her fans were concerned, Sheena was just another one of the TV heroes. However, before we applaud this seemingly enlightened nonsexist attitude, let us look a little deeper. The *reason* she was brought from the comics to the tube was to lure ol' dad to the set when his kids tuned in. He was the one with the money to buy a sponsor's product, and there was no reason to assume that he wouldn't spend a half-hour on Sunday afternoons watching a well-built woman run half-naked through the jungle. Thus, although there were no outright allusions to her gender, Sheena was most definitely a sex object! And the heroine in television took another large step backward!

The final children's show of the year was "My Friend Flicka," a virtual rehashing of "Fury," with the exception that Johnny Washbrook, the horse's young master, lived with his parents, played by Anita Louise and Gene Evans. And so, with Chim and Flicka to send us on our way, we return to the world of adult programming.

Since the full impact of "Gunsmoke," "Wyatt Earp," and "Cheyenne" had not yet made itself felt, producers were still pushing formulae from previous years. "The Man Called X," for instance, was really Ken Thurston (Barry Sullivan) of the CIA. His playground was the world, and his job entailed such assignments as preventing the assassination of a Free Chinese leader, rescuing underground operatives in Czechoslovakia, and other equally tired missions. About the only new twist in the show was that the majority of Thurston's foes were women in clever disguises, a welcome antithesis to the clichéd Mata Hari lady spy. But even they weren't enough to enliven the tired storylines. Equally standard fare was "State Trooper," starring Rod Cameron as modern-day lawman Rod Blake, while "Wire Service" took viewers inside the news-gathering machinery of the International News Service, alternately following the exploits of reporters Mercedes McCambridge, George Brent, and Dane Clark. On the medical front, Macdonald Carey was Dr. Christian, a young and active medical man in a modern metropolis. Based on the radio character played for sixteen years by Jean Hersholt, "Dr. Christian," according to Carey, "is not *Medic*. The emphasis in our story is placed on human problems, not scientific ones." The season's other physician was John Howard, the star of "Dr. Hudson's Secret Journal." Based on the novel by Lloyd C. Douglas, Hudson's concern was also with human rather than medical complications at Center Hospital.

Sadly, the one comparatively novel series of 1956 was also a poorly executed one. With World War II more than a decade removed, Hollywood felt that it was time for something like "Combat Sergeant," the exploits of Sgt. Nelson (Mike Thomas) and Lt. Kruger (Bill Slack) of the North African campaign. Hollywood may have been right, and the show was not without merit. Stock footage from actual battles was carefully and successfully intercut with new material, and war was shown to be a vicious affair. But the program worked hard to foster the impression that Nelson and his men won every encounter with the enemy single-handedly. This ludicrous idea, aggravated by Nazi stereotypes, made the program a bit much to swallow—especially without John Wayne.

Capitulating to that terrible tyrant known as the bandwagon, producers brought forth no less than twelve Adult Westerns in 1957, along with a handful of juvenile series. All of these were drawn from a bagful of pilots, which included the unsold "Fremont the Trailblazer," starring Steve Cochran; "The Sheriff's Wife," with Lori March; and "The Man from Texas," which was to have been the story of Sam Houston. Then there were the shows that did win weekly berths, including "Have Gun Will Travel," one of the few Westerns that would outlast the craze. "Have Gun Will Travel" broke the image that Richard Boone had created for himself in "Medic"—that of an obdurate physician—and replaced it with that of an obdurate adventurer named Paladin. The word *paladin*, of course, describes anyone who undertakes a noble cause. Paladin was a well-educated ex-army officer who lived the strange double life of a wealthy man-about-town in San Francisco and a hired gun in the hinterlands. Boone, a distant nephew of Daniel, was an appropriate choice for the role. A rugged 6'2", he had been an ordnanceman in the Navy, and was well acquainted with guns and other weapons. Thus, the actor was right at home working with Paladin's belt derringer, six-shooters, saddle rifle, and self-styled machine gun. But he was even more at home with the active Paladin:

I guess the word for Dr. Styner was objective. But this Paladin is no mere observer. He's a participant who lives like a king with a need to make the most of every moment, whether he's drinking a glass of wine or hunting somebody down.

Yet, there was something about Paladin's cocksureness that made him more like one of Homer's playful gods than a mortal hero. While this would tend to lessen a viewer's identification with any other character, no one seemed to mind it in Paladin. For, despite his apparent indestructibility, "people like Paladin," Boone explained. "He's an intriguing sort of guy with an air of mystery about him." Coupled with action and interesting plots, the enigma of Paladin, like the smile on Mona Lisa or the hidden secrets of the Great Pyramids, was what kept people coming back week after week.[17]

Another hit in that crowded television season was "Maverick"—a word defined as an independent person—starring James Garner as Bret Maverick and Jack Kelly as his brother Bart, cowardly gamblers who did not wish to serve mankind but to fleece it at every turn. Yet, even in this low occupation there was a cockeyed form of heroism. It stemmed from the fact that the brothers were able to survive from week to week! Typical of their escapades was when Bret and pal Dandy Jim (Elfrem Zimbalist, Jr.) talked hillbilly Noah Perkins (Mike Lane) into challenging the mighty boxer Battling Kruger (Pat Comisky). When the boy backed out, Bret had to take his place. On another occasion, the brothers found themselves broke and in New Orleans. To make money by playing poker on a riverboat, they rescued the shipowner's kidnapped daughter and thus gained passage.

As *TV Guide* accurately noted, the brothers had none of the "rugged individualism, lofty moral principles, lack of humor, fanatical courage, mechanical marksmanship, physical perfection, unflinching honesty, commendable generosity, and all the other attributes of the Western hero." According to producer Roy Huggins, one of the creators of "Cheyenne," these were exactly the characteristics he was trying to discard. "*Maverick* is simply *Cheyenne* turned inside-out," Huggins said.

> All cowboy heroes are Freudian father figures. That's why Gary Cooper, John Wayne, and all the others since William S. Hart have been big guys. If you don't believe it, try to think of a fictional cowboy with a father. On *Maverick*, I wanted to see how many rules we could break and get away with it.[18]

He certainly had the right star for his sixty-minute dose of iconoclasm. James Garner gave at least every appearance of being a hero. Standing 6′3″, with a determined gaze and youthful vigor, Garner came to the show direct from five appearances as a "heavy" in "Cheyenne." More important, however, was the fact that Garner was typecast. "I'm playing me," the actor admitted. "Bret Maverick is lazy; I'm lazy. And I *like* being lazy!" As for the less irresponsible Kelly, he was written into the show when it proved impossible to finish each program on time. One crew was assigned to film his scenes, while another unit was shooting Garner. The result of these efforts was a tongue-in-cheek comedy that

proved to be a breath of fresh air in an increasingly self-righteous environment. And while the show caught on, it would have had to survive with only Kelly and newcomer Roger Moore as Beau Maverick when, three years later, Garner left after suing Warner Brothers—and winning—for breach of contract.

The third blockbuster that season was "Wagon Train," the story of an epic pilgrimage from Missouri to California. Ward Bond starred as Major Seth Adams, the authoritative leader of this westward trek, and Robert Horton was Flint McCullough, a young scout for the pioneers. Produced at a staggering cost of $100,000 per week, "Wagon Train" was a sprawling, well-wrought saga that refused to make concessions to the genre. Horton, for instance, had strong feelings about the way his part had to be played. "Why should I act like a movie cowboy? I'm *not* a movie cowboy, and most of the real cowboys of 1870 weren't either. They were from the East, and a lot of them were well-educated." Bond, meanwhile, was on-hand to serve as a link with the traditional Western persona. According to Horton, "Ward plays Seth the way he's been playing Western heroes for thirty years. If the script says grin, he grins. If it says knock the man down, he knocks the man down. His technique serves him perfectly, but I couldn't use it." Beyond his performance, Bond kept the show from following in the footsteps of "Gunsmoke" and the psychotic Western. When he took the role, the star of over two hundred Western films stated flatly, "Nobody is going to make me play a story with a degenerate in it. Not on a TV show that children are watching." And that was that. After Bond's death in 1961, John McIntyre joined the cast, but the series' basic orientation remained unchanged.

Based on the popular John Ford film *Wagonmaster* (1950)—of which Bond was the star—"Wagon Train" concentrated primarily on the stories of guest stars, such as Bette Davis, John Wayne, Michael Rennie, and Mickey Rooney—all of whom were either joining or leaving the trek and suffering from one problem or another.[19] The situations they faced and the emotions they felt were all credible, and, thus, the pursuant emotional outpourings were also valid. This kept the program consistently sophisticated and engrossing. Of course, there was usually a gunfight or two per episode to please the genre buffs, but these were played down.

The remaining new wave Westerns were, on the whole, a redundant, unimaginative lot. "Trackdown," for example, was a clumsy attempt to break the established Adult Western format. Set in the 1870s, and starring the twenty-six-year-old Robert Culp as Texas Ranger Hoby Gilman, the emphasis in "Trackdown" was

The men of "Wagon Train." From left to right: Frank McGrath,
John McIntire, Terry Wilson, and Robert Fuller.

on intrigue rather than guns and horses. Unfortunately, most of the scripts were not absorbing enough to hold an audience without the traditional Western trappings. In a word, it was well intentioned but dull. In this respect, "Tales of Wells Fargo" was the exact opposite, an entertaining throwback to the simple-minded days of "Hopalong Cassidy." Dale Robertson portrayed Fargo agent Jim Hardie, a man forged of the knight-in-shining-armor mold. In fact, Hardie was such a threadbare and typical character that the role, at first, did not appeal to Robertson:

> I thought there were going to be too many Westerns on TV. I knew of about one hundred unsold test films for Western series. Besides, I had my sights on something else. I was up for *Perry Mason*. Unfortunately, they didn't want to make Mason the kind of character I talk like.

So he did "Wells Fargo" and, despite its very artless—albeit exciting—nature, the show ended up knocking "Maverick" from the number-two spot on the ratings charts. However, the program did have one rather original notion, although it was an option never used. "People don't realize," Robertson said,

> that Wells Fargo was the biggest banking and express agency in the West. They had offices all over the world. If the Western craze begins to wear thin, all we have to do is send Jim Hardie packing off to Rome and we have a brand new show. But where can Wyatt Earp go?

Another successful pair of series' that season were "Colt .45" and "Tombstone Territory." "Colt .45" was about Christopher Colt (Wayde Preston), an undercover agent for the government and son of Sam Colt, the gunmaker who invented the titular firearm. The somewhat more formidable-sounding "Tombstone Territory" centered around the exploits of Sheriff Clay Hollister (Pat Conway), as actually recorded in the pages of a newspaper called *The Tombstone Epitaph*. Both series were only moderately diverting by standards of the time, but they happened to be selling what the public was buying.

Meanwhile, already seeking fresh twists for a rapidly decaying theme, programers came up with "Sugarfoot," the story of an Easterner who went West to become a cowboy. Portraying tenderfoot Tom Brewster was 6'1" Will Hutchins, the only performer among this new breed of Western stars to have a show tailored to his particular acting style. A man of no pretention and who was always at ease, Hutchins played a drifter with a gentle disposition but a strong sense of justice. However, beyond the black-cloud-beneath-a-silver-lining angle was the gimmick that, while drifting from town to town, Sugarfoot also carried on a correspondence course in law. Naturally, Sugarfoot's background and ambition to become an attorney were a source of amusement to rugged Westerners, and Brewster was constantly called upon to tender his value in lead and knuckles. A second hero with a dovish exterior but a core of iron was "The Restless Gun," a series featuring film star John Payne. Payne did his drifting as Vint Bonner, a Civil War veteran with the reputation for being a top gun, but who actually loathed violence. In fact, Bonner was not only against gunplay, but on one occasion went so far as to advise an antagonist, "Look. We're both too old for this kind of foolishness, especially on such a nice summer day." This is certainly not your standard heroic dialogue, and speeches like these were notorious for prompting cries of cowardice, which were inevitably the last words ever uttered by Bonner's opponent.

Speaking of Civil War veterans, such as Bonner and Paladin, the War Between the States was also used as the backdrop for the adventures of Major John Singleton Mosby, a fighting man known to his foes as "The Gray Ghost." Historically, Mosby (Tod Andrews) and his raiders were Confederate soldiers who specialized in daring attacks on Northern positions. While the series tended to exaggerate the indestructibility of Mosby's marauders, there was no overstating their value to the South. As Andrews observed, "Yankees sometimes complain that we're rewriting history, that the South always wins. I have to explain that we're doing the story from Mosby's viewpoint, and that he did carry off a lot of successful raids." Further, Andrews defended the show as being nonpartisan:

Mosby had sincerity, love of country, and a conscience about killing. Since getting interested in Mosby, I've come to have a pretty warm feeling for the South and for the tradition of courage on both sides that made the war the fascinating human struggle it was.

However, none of these higher intentions saved the show from being just another routine action series.

It's quite clear that while these numerous efforts varied in broad or subtle ways concerning plot, they all shared the common element of the hero. Thus, in an effort to blaze entirely new trails in adult programming, "The Californians" did away with even that element of the story, replacing him with the antihero. The antihero, whom we will discuss more fully in chapter 7, is a character of questionable moral fabric. And that's just the breed of cat that held court along the Barbary Coast of the mid-1800s. "The Californians" portrayed San Francisco as a land of vigilantes who earned the right to govern by eliminating all contenders. Actors Adam Kennedy and Sean McClory were the chief practitioners of this autocratic rule and were represented as having the integrity of snakes. Unfortunately, reptile-men have never been marked for a prosperous television life no matter what the ratings say. The program's sponsors, fearful that viewers might accuse them of condoning this sort of arrogance, gave Kennedy and McClory passage on the next stage to unemployment and ushered in clean-living sheriff Matt Wayne (Dick Coogan) to bring order to the Bay area. A highly moral dandy whose worst vice was to cast an occasional eye at the ladies, Wayne transformed "The Californians" from a truly adult experiment to a juvenile travesty. In almost any other medium, be it film, literature, or music, this change would have insulted an audience beyond measure. But the series found its moderate-sized audience unchanged and was cancelled soon thereafter. The stasis of the ratings leads one to wonder if anyone had even noticed the change!

Sadly, "The Californians," in its tidied-up version, found equally deficient fare to keep it company. Geared for the kiddies, the remaining four Westerns of 1957 were abysmal. "Hawkeye and the Last of the Mohicans," based ever so loosely on Cooper, starred John Hart as the paleface scout Hawkeye, and the venerable Lon Chaney, Jr. as his sometimes-faithful Indian companion, Chingachogook. Shot in Canada, the show was drab and uninspired. "Pony Express" suffered from the same lack of visual and scriptural fertility, as did "Sheriff of Cochise," starring John Bromfield as the peacekeeper in contemporary Cochise County, Arizona. In 1959, he would be promoted to "U.S. Marshal"—and the program's title changed accordingly—when Tucson's law-

The rough-hewn mountain men in "The Saga of Andy Burnett." From left to right: Jerome Courtland, Jeff York, and Andrew Duggan. © Walt Disney Productions.

man (Sidney Blackmer) was gunned down. However, given the mass-manufactured milieu from which these series grew, one can acknowledge and forgive them for being quick-buck products. But when this same caliber of material, inspired by the same crash-cash motives, turned up on "Disneyland," the sin cannot be as freely dismissed.

Walt Disney's six-part "Disneyland" presentation "The Saga of Andy Burnett" was a rushed, sloppy production. Jerome Courtland played the mountain man who agreed to escort a group of youngsters from Pittsburgh through Blackfoot Indian territory to a settlement in the West, just north of Pike's Peak. The program was supposed to reach the same heights of popularity as "Davy Crockett" but missed its target through lack of personality in both the players and production. To paraphrase what we said earlier, heroic deeds and adventures without the proper balance of

enthusiasm, risk, muscle, and purpose in the featured player do not a hero make. Without the fortitude and confidence of Crockett, Andy Burnett never had a chance. But these were faults that Disney would rectify with another of his 1957 series, the most exciting youth-oriented hero since "The Lone Ranger."

"Zorro" has had a substantial and distinguished film career. Three movie versions of *The Mark of Zorro*, with Douglas Fairbanks (1920) Tyrone Power (1940), and Frank Langella (1974); a motion picture called *Zorro* (1976), starring Alain Delon; and a trio of serials—all constitute his screen incarnations. But it remained for Disney to come up with a perfect blend of characterization, plot, flamboyance, and action, to make the hero a household word. Guy Williams starred as Don Diego de la Vega, son of the wealthiest *hidalgo* in eighteenth-century California. Posing by day as a mincing fop with no stomach for either commitment or violence, the young Diego slipped into a black costume, cloak, mask, and hat by night to become Zorro, a swashbuckling vigilante who fought Spanish oppression in the New World. The

Some of the men who've played Zorro: Douglas Fairbanks, Tyrone Power, and Frank Langella.

target of his raids was the tyrannical commandant Capt. Manastario (Britt Lomand), and his portly, bumbling aide, Sgt. Garcia (Henry Clavin). Zorro's calling card was a *Z*, which he carved with his rapier on buildings, furniture, and people; the hero's lair, secreted in the side of a mountain, was maintained by the mute servant Bernardo (Gene Sheldon).

Of the screen Zorros that history has judged to be classic, Fairbanks' was the most athletic, but he worked his leaps and stunts until they were no longer relevant to the plot. Power was an actor and, as such, clearly enjoyed contrasting the effeminate Diego with his dynamic alter ego; but he brought little flair to the role. Williams, on the other hand, engaged in dramatic duels and frenzied chases, while he put meat on the bones of Zorro and Diego both. And the end result was that boys all over the country traded in their coonskin caps for chalk-tipped plastic swords—with which they slashed *Z*'s on sidewalks and walls—and Zorro masks and capes. Although the half-hour series was gone after two seasons, it enjoyed a third year on "Walt Disney Presents"— formerly "Disneyland"—as six hour-long adventures.

With "Zorro," a fringe member of the video Western, we conclude our look at that season's contributions to the genre. There would be over a dozen new additions to the field in 1958, but, for the nonce, let's look at television's non-Western heroes.

Zorro (Guy Williams) teams up with mountain man Joe Crane (Jeff York) in the "Zorro" TV series. © Walt Disney Productions.

Guy Williams as Zorro astride his horse Phantom. © Walt Disney Productions.

The sole ancient history lesson came from "Ivanhoe," a series created by the producers of "Robin Hood." The movies' future James Bond, Roger Moore, starred as Sir Walter Scott's immortal medieval English hero, but the proceedings were still drab. The reasons for this were outlined by the actor shortly after the program's demise: "No one seemed to know what we were doing, and we all stumbled about feeling like boy scouts dressed up in armor." Also lacking vitality were the crews of this season's other "novelty" shows: "Harbor Command," with Wendell Corey as a dock-side law enforcer; "The New Adventures of Charlie Chan," starring the great J. Carrol Naish as Carl Derr Bigger's Oriental sleuth; "Scotland Yard," the omnibus program narrated by famed British criminologist Edgar Lustgarten; "Danger is My Business," with Scott Brady as a pilot-for-hire; "O.S.S." featuring Ron Randall as Frank Hawthorn and based on declassified files from the office of Strategic Services; "Casey Jones," boasting movie veteran Alan Hale as the legendary trainman; and three programs set in Africa—"White Hunter," "African Patrol," with John Bentley in Nairobi, and "The Michaels of Africa," a sort of Little House on the Veldt. Indeed, the only impressive gimmick series of the year was "Whirlybirds," a well-acted and photographed show about P.T. (Craig Hill) and Chuck (Kenneth Tobey), a pair of free-lance helicopter pilots. Using their chopper, a vehicle that allowed for more visual and dramatic storylines than the airplane in "Danger is My Business," the fliers chased criminals into forests, hunted down a gorilla escaped from a circus, rescued a child trapped on a precarious mountain peak, and so forth. Another asset of the series was the personalities of the two players. With the solemn Chuck as an anchor, the glib, wise-cracking P.T. offered wry comments about the goings-on, providing substance for the ear as well as for the eye. Unfortunately, viewers seemed to prefer heroes who kept both feet on the ground, and "Whirlybirds" was gone by season's end.

Not unexpectedly, what with the deluge of Westerns and novelty adventures series, new police and detective shows were kept to a minimum. Yet, the sole out-and-out cop entry of the year was a tremendous hit, as Lee Marvin surrendered his tough-guy movie roles for a tough-guy television role as the star of "M-Squad." According to Marvin, "The *M* doesn't stand for anything. It's any dirty job." Hacked from the "Dragnet" mold, "M-Squad" brought realistic police adventure to a Chicago locale. However, the draw was not authenticity, but Marvin himself. His hard-as-nails Lt. Frank Ballinger was everyone's ideal cop, more explosive than the even-tempered Joe Friday and more rugged than the businesslike "Treasury Men in Action." Not that this potent character was entirely to Marvin's liking. For him, the show's first season left much to be desired. "I wanted Ballinger to show some weaknesses occasionally," he complained. "It makes him human. So I told the studio, but they said, 'Well, yeah, maybe, but nobody's ever done it.' So we didn't. You can't change fast in front of an audience. It scared them; too real." When the show caught fire , the producers yielded to Marvin's wishes; he fleshed-out the character, and Ballinger quickly became the most credible cop in television history. But Marvin still wasn't happy, although not because of Ballinger. "I would get out of this series if I could," he said as "M-Squad" entered its second season, adding:

> It's a straight jacket. Do you realize that I'm playing the same character on nineteen-and-a-half hours of film a year? And it gets pretty dull. In a movie, you're on for maybe forty-five minutes, and that's it. The audience doesn't stand much chance of anticipating you. After the second week in a series, they *gotta* anticipate you. And when they do, *adios!*

It's a pity these lofty concerns were not an issue with Marvin's peers, most of whom were not playing cops but

Raymond Burr as Perry Mason. Incidentally, the notations on his desk calendar appear to be stage directions. The folder before him is the Statistical Digest, LAPD.

supersleuths. David Janssen, a bit actor from the movies, scored a mild success with "Richard Diamond," a private eye series in which the hero was introduced to a case through some innocent young lady. For example, on vacation in the mountains, Diamond was called to action by threats aimed at an attractive miss. On another occasion, he was asked to look after a gangster's girl friend. Still another adventure had him approached by a woman who asked Diamond to help clear her fiance of murder—and so it went, week after week. In fact, the only female that the series played down was Diamond's leggy secretary, Sam, in the person of Mary Tyler Moore. Then there was the flip side of the coin, as Frank Lovejoy played a private detective in "Meet McGraw." Unlike Diamond's habitat, McGraw's world was frilled with the kind of characters who hang out in dockside dives, alleyways, and seedy hotels. In short, Lovejoy played a man's man, as opposed to Janssen who was—and remained, even in later series—a ladies' man. Commenting on the lack of women in his series, Lovejoy said. "What we're driving at is a character who would act like a human being in every situation. The women don't fall over McGraw any more than they do over most men in real life."

Leaving behind the gutter-and-glamour world of the television gumshoe, we find drama in the tradition of "Mr. and Mrs. North," as Peter Lawford and Phyllis Kirk appeared in a televersion of *The Thin Man*. Based on the adventures of the sophisticated ex-detective Nick Charles and his wife Nora, the Dashiell Hammett creations had already been brought to the screen in six immortal motion pictures starring William Powell and Myrna Loy. And while Lawford and Kirk exhibited the proper balance of mutual ribbing and serious sleuthing, they were unable to capture the winsome flavor of their distinguished predecessors. Only their pet wire-haired fox terrier managed to hold his own against the movie counterpart. Obviously, it was a near-barren season for the minions of twentieth-century crime-fighting. For, with the exception of "M-Squad," only one other program dealing with justice struck a responsive chord. That series was "Perry Mason." Created by mystery writer Erle Stanley Gardner, "Perry Mason" was the lawyer who never lost a case—something the series' detractors found particularly bothersome. However, this peculiar orientation can be defended in three ways: First, as star Raymond Burr noted: "We don't stack the deck in favor of Perry. Rather, he is judicious in picking his clients. He believes in them, and happens to believe correctly. What would you want us to do? Send an innocent man to the chair?" The second, a more academic approach, is

Peter Lawford and Phyllis Kirk in "The Thin Man."

that the reality of the screen or television hero dictates that he never lose or, if he does, must fall as a martyr. Finally, Perry Mason won all his cases simply because he was the champion of underdogs, ordinary people fighting against a state that was working to prove them guilty of some hideous crime. Thus, Perry's victories were, in a subtle way, the defendant's successful defeat of the proverbial City Hall; strong food for viewer identification, this. Assisting Mr. Burr in his cases was secretary Della Street (Barbara Hale), with Ray Collins featured as Lt. Tragg of homicide and William Talman starring as District Attorney Burger.

As television prepares to enter its second decade of full-scale broadcasting, the hero is removed from simple mimicry of the movie serial and radio characters only in the occasional depth that producers allowed to infuse his character. However, the next ten years would see more dramatic shifts as television itself began to grow up, and the hero started to mirror the fears and growth pains of a nation. And like the world from which these new characters would come, it was to be an exciting time for television.

4

A Search for Identity

*A friend of mine is an FBI agent, and he's no more like
Eliot Ness than I am. They've got so many rules and
regulations it's all he can do to blow his nose.*
　　　　　　　　　—Robert Stack
　　　　　　　　　　Star of "The Untouchables"

Any flood is bound to deposit mud in the public's lap,
and that's exactly what happened in 1958. The Western
deluge continued, prompting *TV Guide* to note:

> With so many Western shows on the air, it's difficult to
> remember which cowboy is plugging what product. And
> that's what worries the sponsors, because there's not much
> point in shelling out all the money, even for a top-rated
> Western, if the commercials aren't getting through to the
> audience.

Accordingly, the 1958 season was to be the last year of
the great Adult Western boom. By 1960, most of the
dozens of sagebrush series that premiered during those
years will, as they say, have bitten the dust. In fact, as in
previous seasons, there were so many Westerns on tap
that many of them were killed after the pilot stage.
Among their number were "Cavalry Surgeon," starring
John Hudson; a teenage Western called "Ricochet,"
with Johnny Weismuller, Jr.; Alex Nicol as "Yankee
Bligh," a New England Pinkerton man who headed West
in 1860; "Snowfire," the story of a pure white stallion;
"Marshal of the Last Frontier," with "Annie Oakley's"
Brad Johnson; the Burt Lancaster productions "Vera

Cruz" and "Apache," based on his motion pictures; and
many others. Strangely, though, and for no apparent
reason, there was also a dramatic return to the police and
private eyes as a foundation for programming this
season. Perhaps, watching the cowboys roll from
Hollywood assemblylines, producers felt that the public
would quickly tire of the genre and look for something
more modern and familiar.

At the moment, however, Westerns were still big
business, and riding high in the saddle—and destined to
outlive the current fad—were "Rawhide" and "The
Rifleman," two programs that had little in common. "The
Rifleman," starring 6'5" ex-major-league baseball
player Chuck Connors as rancher Lucas McCain, was a
Western fantasy. Widower McCain, trying to raise his
young son Mark (Johnny Crawford) on a spread outside
the town of North Fork, was constantly facing rustlers,
bullies, drunks, killers, etc., and allowed his .44 caliber
Winchester to do most of the talking. But the shooting
was usually underplayed or, wherever possible, executed off camera. As Connors opined: "People object to
the emphasis, not the violence itself." On a more
domestic level, the relationship between the jut-jawed
McCain and his preteenage son was one of absolute
warmth and devotion. This gave him a chink in his
armor, which in its identifiable simplicity made him
more credible than most other heroes on the tube. Thus,
while Lucas hadn't the impenetrable emotional shell of a
Cheyenne Bodie, he was a flawed but human hero.

Johnny Crawford and Chuck Connors in "The Rifleman."

actions were not always what they should have been. In one episode, he had five major decisions to make, and made them all wrong. As a result, Favor's men deserted him and he undertook the near-impossible task of continuing the drive alone. Impressed with his courage, the cattlemen rejoined him. When asked if this was a touch of sentimentality on the part of the screenwriters, Warren replied, "No, it was simply a case of 1866 guts on the part of Favor."

Another successful series, as handy at destroying clichés as it was in calling attention to its leading player, was Gene Barry's "Bat Masterson." He was the only TV character who, for example, got involved with rustlers not for justice's sake, but because he had won several steers in a poker game and was looking to protect his winnings. In brief, he was an antihero. And according to Barry, he and the posturing man of substance were much alike. "He's elegant, dapper, and colorful, with human failings and human attributes. He's not just a one-dimensional saddle-type, but a sophisticated gentleman of the West." Thus, Barry, who described his own self as "sensitive, very determined, articulate, and always well dressed," slipped right into the part. Beyond his sartorial splendor and polished manners, however, Bat was excellent with a gun and very handy with a silver-tipped

Contrarily, "Rawhide" was the closest that television had ever come to creating an authentic sweat-and-blood Western. The series made no attempt to embellish the basic format of man-against-the-West to encompass any of the more romantic notions mentioned above. The continuing story of a cattle drive, "Rawhide" featured Eric Fleming as Gil Favor, the cattle boss, and Clint Eastwood as his scout, Rowdy Yates. Discussing why his show was different from other TV Westerns, producer Charles Marquis Warren said,

> With us, the herd is primary. We're always up against the elements, and we never leave them entirely behind. For instance, the *Wagon Train* people come across their exploits and suddenly, the wagon train disappears while they tell their story.

Nor were Favor and Yates typical television heroes. Their sole purpose in life was to escort the cattle from one point to another. "With the acute beef shortage, and a nation starving after the Civil War," Warren said, "if it came to a choice between men and beeves, the beeves won." When, for example, Indians charged the cowboys ten head of cattle for permission to pass through their land, Favor, "gave 'em the beeves, shot down the Indians at night, and stole the beeves back." Of course, Favor's

Robert Loggia as Elfego Baca in the serialized presentation "Elfego Baca and the Mustangers." © Walt Disney Productions.

Elfego Baca is drawn into a fight by cowhand Buffalo (Guinn Williams) in a scene from Friendly Enemies at Law. © *Walt Disney Productions.*

Tom Tryon as Texas John Slaughter. © *Walt Disney Productions.*

cane that was always in his possession. His ability to use these weapons and get tough without shedding or mussing his chic exterior made Bat unique, if not entirely, credible. Even the Lone Ranger tore his vestments on occasion.

Only three of the remaining fifteen Western series met with the public's approval that season—two of them appearing on "Walt Disney Presents," and the other featuring a young man destined to become one of the cinema's great superstars. "Elfego Baca" and "Texas John Slaughter" were both miniseries presented on the Disney anthology program. Robert Loggia, who went on to play one of the author's favorite television heroes in 1967, starred in the four-part "Elfego Baca" show, the story of a Mexican-American lawman who was also known as "El Gato, The Cat." Allegedly the possessor of nine lives, Baca lost an average of two lives per week, as he tried to keep the peace in Tombstone, Arizona, without resorting to violence. "Texas John Slaughter" had no such qualms about fisticuffs or gunplay. A crack shot, he didn't hesitate to enforce his will with lead. Author Tom Tryon (*The Other, Harvest Home,* and *Lady*) portrayed the real-life Western hero. Finally, a historical character in timbre if not in name, was the 1890s bounty hunter of "Wanted: Dead or Alive." An unscrupulous character-type from the United States' past, bounty hunter Josh Randall was a man who checked the wanted posters in whatever town he happened to be, tracked down and captured the culprit, and returned to claim the reward. Less interested in upholding the law than in collecting a sizeable recompense for his efforts, the nihilistic Randall provided an excellent vehicle for movie rebel Steve McQueen. Coming to the role from such theatrical films as *Never Love a Stranger* (1958) and *The Blob* (1959), and following it with the smash hits *The Magnificent Seven* (1960) and *The Great Escape* (1963), the small, 5′11″ actor held his own in a television West populated by such physical giants as Arness, Connors, and Walker, by maintaining an image of rugged inflapability. A self-assured loner, the antiheroic McQueen, with his famous sawed-off shotgun—like its owner, a symbol of individualistic nonconformity—were a welcome change-of-pace in an overly pristine West.

As for the rest of this season's starters, to say they were routine is to be generous. The series were either rehashes of established hits or ill-conceived novelties: there were "The Texan," starring 6′3″ Rory Calhoun as a drifting gun-for-hire; "Lawman," with John Russell as Marshal Dan Troop of Laramie, Wyoming; "Rough Riders," which was not, as one might logically expect, about

Teddy Roosevelt's hardy band of Spanish-American War heroes, but the story of two Union veterans (Kent Taylor and Peter Whitney) and one ex-rebel (Jan Merlin), who scoured the Dakota Badlands as knights-errant; "Twenty-Six Men," with former serial star Tristram Coffin as the head of the Arizona Rangers, circa 1900; "Northwest Passage," starring Keith Larsen, Buddy Ebsen, and Don Burnett as a group of colonists who fought the British during the French and Indian War; "Cimarron City," an Oklahoma town of the early 1800s, with George Montgomery as Matt Rockford, a benevolent cattle baron who became mayor; Peter Breck as Clay Culhane, a reformed gunfighter in "Black Saddle"; Rex Reason, alias Adam MacLean, the "Man Without a Gun"; former "Range Rider" Jock Mahoney as "Yancy Derringer," the ex-Confederate officer who, with his aide Pahoo (X. Brands), worked as a secret agent in New Orleans; Jeff Morrow as Bart McClelland of the "Union Pacific," Richard Carlson, fresh from "I Led Three Lives," as Col. Ranald McKenzie, head of "McKenzie's Raiders," a group of undercover agents patrolling the Mexican border; and "Jefferson Drum," featuring Jeff Richards as a Western newspaper editor and all-around good guy. It was the kind of season that might have

Rory Calhoun as the Texan.

fostered a surge in America's book-buying habits had it not been for a handful of cops and private eyes, and one suboceanic adventurer.

This might be a good time to pause and look briefly at that amorphous element called the Public Fancy. There isn't a producer, novelist, composer, or illustrator who can predict trends in his particular field. For example, the audience for a property like *Jaws* can be built by spending millions of dollars to promote it from hardcover novel to paperback book to film and to spin-off merchandising. Yet even then there's no guarantee of success. Consider the fate of books like *The Greatest* by Muhammad Ali; films like *Jonathan Livingston Seagull* (1973) or *The Great Gatsby* (1974); television shows like "Beacon Hill" (1975). All were publicized until potential audiences were thoroughly familiar with each commodity, but they were simply and ultimately not what anyone was buying! At another time, the same obscurity might just have easily been the fate of *Jaws*.

No one anticipated the popularity of the Adult Western. Accordingly, producers who got there first or with something that the public wanted—that elusive blend of star, situation, and setting—had hits on their hands. The remaining series died. And yet, almost paradoxically, there *is* a constant in television, a mode with a remarkable track record: the police and detective program. Looking at these shows from "Rocky King" to "Kojak," we find several invariable ingredients: First, the main character cannot be detoured from a path of moral justice, embellishing the Letter of the Law only with his inherent compassion. If he is led from the straight and narrow, he must pay a severe price. Second, he is tough and confident, and does not generally pamper himself with excessive physical comforts. The public likes a hero who isn't afraid to roll up his shirt-sleeves and get down to the business at hand. While the hero may sport a touch of the exotic, such as a yacht or penthouse residence, he must quickly leave this locale or risk losing his largely middle-class audience. Third, he works without gimmicks. The actors who have portrayed such characters as James Bond and Batman compete with the frills that utterly dominate their scripts. And, though these two heroes are well liked, they constitute the only long-term successes in their field, as opposed to the great many cops and detectives who have been popular over the years. The emphasis must be on people. Finally, he is contemporary. It is easiest for a viewer to identify with a character who shares with him the same moral, political, and cultural environment. When any of these four elements were ignored, the character invariably failed. Following them, producers have almost always had hits. And, thus, we account for the success and abundance of police and private-eye shows over the years.

There were three such blockbusters that season, and while they all fit the aforementioned categories they accented those of the four aspects that best suited their particular format. The most popular of these was "77 Sunset Strip," a Hollywood detective garrison manned by Efrem Zimbalist, Jr., Roger Smith, Eddie Byrnes, and, later, Richard Long. Originally, the series was a feature-length film entitled "Girl on the Run," with an emphasis on the glittering Los Angeles locale. Unfortunately, neither the producers or the studio was enthusiastic about the film's long-distance box-office legs. But they liked the idea of detectives operating on the lively and legendary strip of Sunset Boulevard, and this film became the show's first episode. Succeeding adventures were usually of a local nature, focusing on gamblers, murderers, or underworld doings, alternately putting Stuart Bailey (Zimbalist) or Jeff Spencer (Smith) on the case. The twenty-six-year-old Byrnes portrayed Kookie—formally Gerald Lloyd Kookson III—a hip and comb-conscious parking-lot attendant who became so popular that, in 1961, he became a full-fledged partner

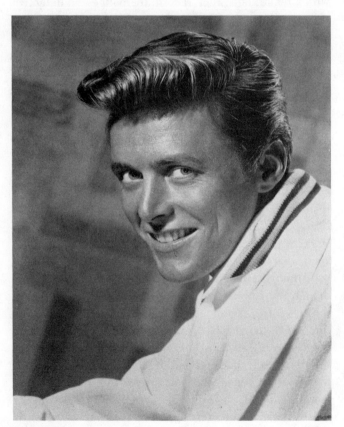

Edd Byrnes as Kookie from "77 Sunset Strip."

of the sleuthing team and was replaced in the lot by Robert Logan.

One of the problems faced by any actor, whether he is playing a detective, cowboy, or movie monster, is to find a way of bringing what performers call their own "equipment" to bear: experiences, physique, emotions, and so forth. For Smith, this was a particularly bothersome aspect of the Jeff Spencer character. "When I first started the show," he said,

> I just couldn't picture myself as a detective. I thought all detectives wore trench coats and scowled like George Raft. So I went around frowning all the time. Then I thought, what if *I* had gone into the private eye business? I conceivably might enjoy it. So I began to smile and be myself, and my fan mail doubled!

While this approach is entirely valid where Smith and Spencer were concerned, a vivid persona is not one of the four concrete requisites in our formula for hits. Take, for example, another of this year's hits, *"Naked City."* Here were characters not unlike Joe Friday and Frank Smith: all business with little time to doff their trench coats, smile, or rise from the grime of the criminal element in which they worked. Based on the excellent Mark Hellinger-Jules Dassin film (1948) of the same name, "Naked City" recounted the exploits of New York City policemen Lt. Dan Muldoon (John McIntire) and (James Franciscus), who were replaced by Det. Lt. Mike Parker (Horace McMahon), Sgt. Frank Arcaro (Harry Bellaver), and Det. Adam Flint (Paul Burke) in the show's second season. Muldoon's death—actually McIntire's move to "Wagon Train"—was responsible for the change.

Filmed on location in Manhattan, each program told "one of the eight million stories in the Naked City," with an emphasis on the stark brick-and-gutter atmosphere of the metropolis. This bent was not far removed from "Dragnet's" approach to police drama, with the sole exception that Los Angeles was presented to us through Friday's eyes, his running commentary giving it a human touch. "Naked City" was not unlike New York itself: cold and distant. Indeed, the exterior scenes were staged primarily in long shots to make the city a part of every activity. Although critics carped that this was done almost to the point of making the players subservient to the setting, it was, in fact, the very essence of the program. Our heroes were on a treadmill, covering ground and doing their duty, but facing the fact that the city was everything, with crime an indigenous part of it. Thus, what "Rawhide" and "Wanted: Dead or Alive" did for the West, presenting downbeat reality in lieu of idealistic myth, "Naked City" did for the cops 'n' robbers genre.

Craig Stevens (top), Lola Albright, and Herschel Bernardi of "Peter Gunn."

Lloyd Bridges in familiar territory. This photograph was taken after "Sea Hunt" had ended its long run.

This is not to say that there wasn't room for a romantic sleuth like Peter Gunn. Gunn (Craig Stevens) was a private investigator who hung out at *Mother's*, a waterfront bar where lady-aide Edie Hart (Lola Albright) worked as a singer. Herschel Bernadri portrayed his police contact, Lt. Jacoby. Producer Blake Edwards (*Return of the Pink Panther*) saw Gunn as

a present day soldier of fortune who has found himself a gimmick that pays him a very comfortable living. The gimmick is trouble. People who have major trouble will pay handsomely to get rid of it, and Peter Gunn is a man who will not only accept the pay but do something about it. He knows every element of the city, from cops to crooks. He also, of course, has his soft side and will occasionally take on a charity job for free.

Thus, if "Naked City" represents the root of our genre flower, with lawmen winding their way through the dirt and teeming mites of the underground, and "77 Sunset Strip" the slick stalk, mixing white-washed visions of crime with a glamorous view of detective work, then "Peter Gunn" is the blossom, the colorful world of the suave, fairy-tale hero.

Unfortunately, most producers were less concerned with the concepts behind new series than with the amount of violence they could cram into a single episode. Mickey Spillane's "Mike Hammer" was a prime example. The renowned mystery writer admits that he "just took the money and went home," and the program suffered because of it. The new writers came up with nothing more than situations that led star Darren McGavin from one beating to another. McGavin industriously made the most of what meat his character had, but the stock plots got the better of him. This is the same problem that plagued Meade Martin as "The Rookie Cop," set in Kansas City; Lee Tracy in "New York Confidential"; Howard St. John as New York City's "The Investigator"; Don Megowan as counterintelligence agent David Harding in "Counterspy"; George Nader as the second "Ellery Queen," which was broadcast live from New York; and Robert Beatty in the Scotland Yard series "Dial 999."

As in previous years, there were enterprising filmmakers who gave viewers a half-hour of programming that struck off in new directions with fresh concepts and interesting premises. While a handful of these programs were stronger in concept than in execution—such as "Rescue 8," with Jim Davis and Lang Jeffries as members of the rescue squad of the Los Angeles Fire Department; "Flying Doctor," with Richard Denning; and "Man with a Camera," starring Charles Bronson as Mike Kovac, an ex-WWII combat photographer who went to work taking pictures for the police—a few shows came up with the crucial blend of innovation and enthusiasm that inspired people to tune in.

Lloyd Bridges had been costarred in such excellent motion pictures as *High Noon* (1952) and *The Rainmaker* (1956), before donning aqualung and swim suit to become Mike Nelson in television's immortal "Sea Hunt." A program like "Sea Hunt" is frustrating for performers, not because of the role, but because of the sensibilities behind it. Bridges had played opposite Gary Cooper, Katharine Hepburn, and Burt Lancaster in hugely prestigious films, yet it was a low-budget weekly series that made his name a household word. Why? The answer lies in simple numbers. An average motion picture is considered a huge success if it grosses fifteen million dollars—that represents roughly six million paid customers. In television, six million viewers amounts to a paltry ratings score of approximately ten—less than half of what a program needs to be considered even a

mild success. This is one reason that movie stars who are potent box-office theatrically often "die" in television series. Their fans are not nearly legion enough to make a dent in the television ratings. Which also serves to underline the fact that in video it's the idea that lures viewers, and not the star.

The concept for "Sea Hunt" began with producer Ivan Tors, a man who went on to specialize in oceanic adventure series such as "Flipper" and "Primus"—both of which we'll examine later. Mike Nelson was a troubleshooting skin and scuba diver whose talents took him to any body of water where people needed help. This included government assignments, such as rescuing a Soviet scientist who was trapped in a minisub, or recovering the nose cone of an ICBM rocket, or private jobs like diving into a flooded Wyoming coal mine to find out what caused the blast. Indeed, what Tors found perplexing about "Sea Hunt" was not creating tasks for Nelson, but keeping the show from becoming water-

Jungle Jim.

logged. "We weren't sure, at first, how much underwater stuff we could get away with," the producer said in a *TV Guide* interview, "but we soon found out that that was what the audience wanted: water, water, and more water." That was the hook, the exotic novelty, and it was also the reason that the program's budget varied. When episodes could be filmed in studio tanks, costs were as low as $25,000. When Tors took his crew on location to Silver Springs, Florida, the Bahamas, or even California's Catalina Island, the price tag doubled. But the show proved a gold mine for its creators, and nearly twenty years after its debut the series is still in rerun syndication.

Like Mike Nelson's subsea playground, one of the world's lushest geographical sites is the jungle, which returned to television in "Jungle Jim," sharing an audience with reruns of "Sheena" and "Ramar." Based on the comic-strip character and popular film series, "Jungle Jim" starred ex-movie-Tarzan Johnny Weissmuller, who shed his loin cloth for a pith helmet in what one critic accurately described as *"Tarzan"* with clothes on." With his prank-pulling chimp associate Timba, the African adventurer prowled the bush country in search of wrongs to right. Better it would have been had Tarzan himself reached the tube. Three pilots were made that year—all of them starring Gordon Scott, the ape-man's finest impersonator. Sadly, these became tied up in red tape over rights to the character, and were ultimately edited into a single narrative and released theatrically as *Tarzan and the Trappers*.

Meanwhile, another comic-strip hero, Steve Canyon, made the transition from printed page to television. In an appropriate bit of type-casting, the intrepid Air Force Colonel was portrayed by Purple Heart winner Dean Fredricks, an actor with an uncanny resemblance to his four-color counterpart. Even more fascinating, however, was the effect that Fredricks had on the strip's creator, Milton Caniff. "Loyal *Steve Canyon* newspaper fans probably expect to see only that which they personally read into the strip," Caniff wrote in a 1958 *TV Guide* article.

I believe, however, that the TV character enables them to better round out the man. I say this because, in viewing the series, I personally have a new multi-dimensional view of the personality on my drawing board. This is an entirely unexpected personal reaction.

However, not enough of the uninitiated public was impressed with Fredricks of Col. Canyon to keep the series airborne. And joining it in oblivion that year were "Jack London's Captain Grief," with Maxwell Reid as David Grief of the *Rattler*; "Adventures of the Seahawk," about a floating governmental electronics lab stationed in the Caribbean and run by John Howard as Commander Hawk; "Rocky Jones," with Richard Crane skirting the globe in his orbital jet; and "The Invisible Man," a contemporization of H. G. Wells. Tangentially, it is an irony of the medium that, unlike even the shabbiest of motion pictures—which are occasionally telecast in the small hours of the night—these series will go unseen for the remainder of recorded history. Perhaps its just as well, given their dubious quality. However, it's a pity that no national archive exists to at least preserve, for posterity, these relics of a unique latter-twentieth-century art form.

In the television business, broadcasters may demand big advertising dollars only for hits, so there was considerable house-cleaning in 1959, as a total of forty-two new adventure series were shuffled in to replace the dead weight. A dozen of these new programs were Westerns, while another twenty new shows featured one or another branch of contemporary law enforcement. Of this latter grouping, several efforts proved at once that they were destined for an early grave. The highly touted, "D. A.'s Man," a Jack Webb effort, confirms what we said earlier: a creative approach that well served a locale like Los Angeles won't necessarily survive a transposition to New York. Following the "Dragnet" formula of drawing material from police files, the series featured hoods who muscled in on small businesses, murdered bookies, and swindled other hoods; standing between them and utter criminal chaos was John Compton as James Horan, a newspaperman and undercover agent investigating crime for the New York D. A.'s office. Hard-hitting, ala Webb? Yes. A gripping tapestry of a two-hundred-year-old city? No. Webb might just as well have delivered "Dragnet" reruns for all the credibility his new series was able to muster. And speaking of yesterday's soup warmed over, properties that richly deserved the axe were Ray Milland as private investigator "Markham"; Macdonald Carey as Philadelphia lawyer Herbert Marris in "Lock-Up"; Lyle Bettger as Driscoll and Harold J. Stone as Kennedy in "The Grand Jury"; Victor Jory as Det. Lt. Howard Finucane and Pat McVey as his reporter-sidekick Ben Andrews on a San Diego beat in "Manhunt"; David Hedison trying on the old James Mason film role as an international spy in "Five Fingers"; Ralph Meeker's sleuthing provost sergeant in the Hawaii-based "Not For Hire"; private eye Rod Cameron with the fancy phone number of "Coronodo-Nine"; Stephen Roberts as Bill Masters and Ed Stroll as Marion Collier, the "Congressional Inves-

Gordon Scott as the would-be TV Tarzan.

tigators"; Philip Carey as the hard-boiled Raymond Chandler dick "Philip Marlowe"; and, in a massacre, the "Four Just Men," starring Dan Dailey as the American do-gooder Tim Collier, Vittorio De Sica as his Italian counterpart Ricco Poccari, Richard Conte as Frenchman Jeff Ryder, and, representing the philanthropic British, Jack Hawkins as Ben Manfred. A final flop was somewhat more inventive as Dennis Morgan portrayed gadget-laden private eye Dennis Chase of "21 Beacon Street." This early "Mission: Impossible" prototype was clever but lavished too much attention on technical gimmicks, about which the audience of 1959 could have cared less. Want a safe cracked? Chase did, so he rented an apartment above the room where the safe was located, placed his camera in a ventilator shaft, used mirrors and a telephoto lens to zoom in on the owner as he worked the tumblers, and came away with the combination. Ingenious, but the camera was the hero—not Chase.

Despite these modest efforts, the season was not entirely barren for minions of the law, as a number of fine actors appeared in detective programs of considerable merit. Foremost among these was the biggest hit of 1959, the weekly adventures of Eliot Ness and "The Untouchables." The series, which was first seen in 1958 as a two-part drama on the "Desilu Playhouse," was less a television program than a social phenomenon. Set in Chicago of the 1930s, "The Untouchables" was filled with Italian mobsters whose presence prompted righteous indignation on the part of Italo-Americans who claimed that they were all being shown as having underworld connections. Concurrently, the sponsor found his product disappearing en route to sales points, or collecting dust in warehouses across the nation. Suspecting criminal influence, the producers ordered the ethnic surnames changed, and, the series' glamour thus dissipated, it quickly fell from favor with the public. This says something about both Hollywood stereotypes and taste—not to mention the impact of the show on those "boycotted" areas of commerce. Unfortunately, to do this subject justice would require a book in itself.

The Untouchables were so-named simply because they couldn't be bribed or bought. As producer Quinn Martin described the men and his program:

It's a cliche, but the man who lives by violence generally dies by violence, but not specifically *because* he lives by violence. He winds up defeated because there are men like Eliot Ness and what the newspapers called his 'Untouchables': men of unquestioned integrity, who happened to believe in law and order and who couldn't be brought over to any other way of thinking.

Heading this team of four (Anthony George, Nicholas

Robert Stack as Eliot Ness in "The Untouchables."

Geogiade, Jerry Paris, and Abel Fernandez)—pared from the seven in real life due to budgetary considerations—was forty-year-old Robert Stack as Ness. As fine as Stack was, the role of Ness was not easily won. Speaking candidly, he admits that "Martin told me I was third choice for the part. They had Van Heflin lined up, but he conked out to do a picture. Then they tried to get Van Johnson." When he, too, became unavailable, Stack got the part. And he gave the Federal agent precisely the gutsy, low-keyed personality the stories demanded. Thus, whether he was involved with Al Capone (Neville Brand), bootleg liquor, price-fixing, or protection rackets, Ness couldn't be fazed or deterred from his chosen course. Nor were he and his men afraid to use their guns when necessary. In fact, lead was sprayed with such remarkable vitality on both sides of the law that "The Untouchables" must be deemed the most aggressive and violent program in television history. But the series was not in business to pull any punches and was true in spirit, if not always in fact, to an extremely brutal period of American history. If it bowed to sensationalism on occasion—by gassing men to death in their cars, or shoving peoples' heads into incinerators—this was only a concession to popular taste.[20]

Another high-quality effort in the crime genre was the Robert Taylor series filmed as "Captain of the Detectives" but aired as simply "The Detectives." Assisting Det. Holbrook (Taylor) in his fight against crime were three lieutenants: Jim Conway (Lee Farr) of Homicide, a young man of idealism and *joie de vivre*; the hard-bitten, cigar-chomping Johnny Russo (Tige Andrews) of Burglary; and Otto Lindstrom (Russ Thorson), an old-timer of Bunco, and a man who knew all the ropes and angles. In 1961, future-Batman Adam West would replace Russ Thorson in the lineup. Not an extraordinary series in terms of plot or pacing, the show relied on its excellent cast to give the stories body. And since the emphasis was on the deductive abilities of these plainclothes characters, rather than on shoot-'em-up confrontations, there was at least material with which they could work. Surprisingly, however, the late Taylor's attitude toward the show was less than enthusiastic. A veteran of over seventy motion pictures, he once said,

I have no illusions whatsoever of contributing anything artistic to the medium. Quite frankly, I am going into television largely because of the money involved. But I'll do the best job I can. I like to walk onto a set, do my job as best I know how, and go home.

John Cassavetes felt rather differently about his show "Staccato." In it, he played Johnny Staccato, a jazz pianist turned private eye, who operated from a Greenwich Village dive. Eduardo Cianelli portrayed the proprietor of the hangout, a place where various personal crimes always had a way of occurring. Unfortunately, "Staccato" was an overt reworking of the "Peter Gunn" format—a fact that colored the opinions of critics and viewers alike. However, in all fairness to Cassavetes, who really believed in the program and defended it to anyone who would listen, he gave the role an almost frantic enthusiasm, something that was largely lacking from Craig Stevens' very businesslike Peter Gunn.

Another pair of rough-and-tumble detective series that premiered in 1959 were "The Lawless Years" and Mike Connors' "Tightrope." "The Lawless Years," like "The Untouchables," was centered around the Prohibition Era and detailed the exploits of one Sgt. Ruditsky (James Gregory). Ruditsky himself served as the program's technical advisor and part-time casting director: he contacted old gangster associates to portray criminals in the series. His only stipulation in helping to bring these stories to the screen was that they be told the way they happened. Although the producers eliminated such specifics as stabbings with ice picks and hot pokers being thrust into people's faces, all the general forms of violence were retained, along with the attendant crimes. In short, it was Ruditsky's spoken intention to accurately re-create a time when men were men. Echoing the comments made by Robert Stack in this chapter's epigraph, he said that "the law today is too interested in preserving an individual's rights and not enough interested in wading in and cleaning up the gangland mess that still exists." He went on to state that most gangsters were "physical cowards. The only time they were brave was when three of them at once could get you with a gun held at the back of your neck."

Happily or irresponsibily—whatever your preference—"Tightrope" had none of these higher aspirations, although it did have an involving premise. It was the job of Mike Connors' nameless, fast-talking, wench-loving undercover operative to infiltrate and destroy criminal operations. The title refers to that thin line between right and wrong he was constantly walking. The show played on a very basic appeal in any heroic drama—the idea of one man versus overwhelming odds and winning. However, as producer Clarence Greene was quick to point out: "This is not just the story of a guy who outsmarts the hoods. He's a man with an inner conflict, a dedicated man, a lonely man who goes ahead despite the limbo he lives in." Still, *TV Guide* felt—and not without justification—that this attitude was gilding the lily, covering up the fact that "Tightrope" existed primarily as a showcase for violence. "In *Tightrope*," they wrote, "there's enough firepower to have assisted the Marine Corps greatly in the full-scale invasion of Tarawa." And they had a point. For example, the following weapons were seen in just the first seven episodes of *Tightrope*: three sawed-off shotguns; fourteen .32 caliber snub-nosed police revolvers; two army-issue .45 caliber automatic pistols; one Thompson sub-machine gun; one .25 caliber Italian Beretta automatic pistol; four tear-gas guns; one razor; twelve switch-blades; four pairs of brass knuckles; two hypodermic needles; and five gallons of theatrical blood. Yet, despite what we shall call the show's "exuberance," Connors felt strongly about his character—one that had particular meaning for him. "My dream, as a child, was to become a criminal lawyer in the good old sense. Then I discovered that there weren't many Clarence Darrows in this day and age." So he decided to invent one. Connors' "Tightrope" agent, as was his later character Mannix, was a character of strength and virtue, despite the very negative influence of his surroundings. Unfortunately, and despite consistently high ratings, "Tightrope" was dropped by the sponsor after its first season. The reason? They did not want to be associated with a program that seemed to sanction violence. Which brings us to the question we raised in the beginning of this text about the effect of TV violence on young viewers.

There are, and will always be, rational arguments for and against television violence. The advocates of such fare claim that with the proper storyline, the vicious struggles of an Eliot Ness or Sgt. Ruditsky can serve as a catharsis to the viewer's own unchanneled hostilities. These people are also correct in observing that there are more atrocities committed on the nightly news than on any television adventure program. The antiviolence spokesmen maintain that violence inspires like action in young viewers. In essence, this is the same argument that dogs at the question of pornography. Will seeing a stag film inspire a male to run out and assault a woman; or will the movie satisfy his sexual appetite in the form of a fantasy and possibly prevent a rape? The answer, no matter what the psychiatrists say, is that it depends on the individual. Violence must be considered in the same light. What the argument really comes down to is the question of censorship. Is it the responsibility of programmers to act as ethical watchdogs for their viewers? The answer is *no*. Television is its own moral monitor, a truly marvelous invention that comes equipped with a device known as the "on-off" switch. When a viewer finds his personal values affronted by the tube, he has every right to turn it off, but not to deny other viewers whatever form of legal entertainment they desire. When it reaches the point, as it did in Philadelphia in 1976, that NBC affiliate KYW refused to air the popular film *Dirty Harry*, deeming it unsuitable for the public, then we must question not only the product, but the medium's role in society as well. However, so as not to create an undue stir with sponsors or public, most producers—unlike the men behind "Tightrope"—prefer to nestle their fare somewhere between the extremes of violence and abject domestication. This, for example, was the level that "77 Sunset Strip" had achieved, as did the 1959 season's imitations of that hit, "Bourbon Street Beat" and "Hawaiian Eye."

The late Richard Long and Andrew Duggan were the detectives on New Orleans' "Bourbon Street Beat." They were involved with much the same sort of business as their Sunset Strip counterparts, but without the youth-oriented lure of a Kookie-type character, or the glittering Hollywood locale. Without denying that the French Quarter has exotic appeal, it lacked the airy pulse of Sunset Boulevard, and "Bourbon Street Beat" expired early in 1960. "Hawaiian Eye," on the other hand, *had* the "77 Sunset Strip" elements, with sunny Hawaii doubling for Los Angeles; "Kookie" present in the person of young nightclub singer Cricket Blake (Connie Stevens); and Tom Lapoka (Robert Conrad) and Tracy Steele (Anthony Eisley) as the free-wheeling Spencer and somber Bailey, who operated from an hotel suite. "Hawaiian Eye" also had an advantage over its brethren in that it refused to take itself too seriously. Indeed, it was to this "light quality" that director Mark Sandrich, Jr. attributed the series' success: "This show is not the grim, heavy-handed, tough-guy kind. The scenery is beautiful and besides, everybody wants to go to Hawaii. So we play it strictly on that light vacation level."

Another detective show paced with a less-than-serious attitude was the Blake Edwards production of "Mr. Lucky." John Vivyan portrayed this sleuth, based on the 1943 Cary Grant film and baked from the "Peter Gunn" dough. The owner of a gambling and restaurant yacht, Lucky was a smooth and erudite adventurer who used his mitts when necessary but was foremost a man of high principle. Although it was never clearly defined, he lived by a gambler's code, which presumably meant that he would hold fast to his word, whether it was given to the law or to a criminal. Assisting Lucky in his various underworld escapades was Ross Martin as Andamo and Pippa Scott as Maggie Shank-Rutherford.

Lucky's elegant world of gentlemanly crime, involving complex swindles, high-class robberies, and an occasional murder, was not to be found in the final law-and-order programs of 1959—"Brenner" and "This Man Dawson." "This Man Dawson" was routine cops versus criminals pap, starring Keith Andes, but "Brenner" treated audiences to a revolutionary concept in police programming. Instead of concentrating on the action element, it emphasized the temperaments and values of the titular father and son detective team. Ed Binns was featured as the elder Roy Brenner, a hard-nosed, by-the-book man on the plainclothes Confidential Squad, and James Broderick was seen as his son Ernie, an emotional man who believed in bending the rules to accommodate human error and sentiment. And, as one might have expected, their most trying cases were those that involved their peers, as when an ex-cop became a gambler and lured suckers into fixed games, or an officer grew overanxious and began framing people in order to make arrests and win a promotion. Although the screenwriters frequently reduced Roy and Ernie to mere philosophical soapboxes, the show's overall quality was never compromised: "Brenner" refused to court unreality or make room for genre clichés. Accordingly, the program was short-lived and has been unjustly neglected in this era dominated by "Naked City" and "The Untouchables."

Then there were the Westerns, four of which clicked and nine of which died. The casualties: "Overland Trail," with William Bendix and Doug McClure as Kelly and Flip, owners of a stageline; "Bronco," starring Ty Hardin as an ex-Confederate captain who became a scourge of the lawless in Texas; "Johnny Ringo," a gunman turned sheriff in the person of Don Durant, who warned the locals on his first day in town: "The next man I find wearing a gun better know how to use it."; "The Man from Blackhawk," with Robert Rockwell as an insurance-company investigator in late-nineteenth-century Chicago, and a man who didn't scare: "I never saved enough money to afford it," he once informed an antagonist; "Hotel de Paree," with Earl Holliman's ex-con Sundance—"Where's the depth to the hero who is one hundred percent good?" Holliman declared—who used his gunfighting skills, also according to the actor, "to do something good *not* because it was morally good, but because there was something in it for him!"; Scott Brady's Western private eye known as "Shotgun Slade"; Joel and son Jody McRea as the sheriff and deputy of "Wichita Town"; Michael Ansara as Buckhart, a New Mexican U.S. Deputy Marshal of the 1800s in "Tales of the Plainsman," about an Harvard-educated Apache whose job it was to heal the wounds between Indian and paleface; and "The Swamp Fox," a "Walt Disney Presents" feature with Leslie Nielsen as South Carolina's immortal General Francis Marion, a master of anti-British guerilla warfare in 1776. Making up for these disasters, however, was "Bonanza," a series that fast became a television fixture. This continuing saga of the Cartwright family starred Canadian actor Lorne Greene as widower Ben Cartwright, the clan patriarch with a strong concern for family and land. Little Joe (Michael Landon) was the youngest of the boys and the hotblood; Hoss (Dan Blocker), the strong sensitive, three-hundred-pound restraining influence; and Adam (Pernell Roberts), the thoughtful, balanced brother. Together, the men ran their 100,000-acre Ponderosa, a timberland on the outskirts of Virginia City, a town in the middle of Nevada's Comstock Lode country. This, of course, was the site of the most valuable deposit of silver ore ever discovered (1859).

Bonanza differed from the majority of television Western series in that it shied away from the philosophy that life favors the underdog. Instead, it paid close attention to the love between these four strong men and how they lived for each other as well as for the land. As Landon rightly remarked, "When you get right down to it, the strongest attachments are between men: fathers and brothers. It all helps take a Western out of the "yup" and "nope" kind of thing." "Bonanza" ran until 1974, weathering Roberts' retirement from the series in 1965 and Blocker's death in 1972.

Rounding out the season's horse operas were "The Deputy," "Laramie," and "The Rebel," each one distinctive in their own way. "The Deputy" brought screen great Henry Fonda to the home screen as Simon Fry, a marshal of the Arizona Territory in 1880. Unfortunately, he appeared in only one of every three episodes, leaving the title deputy, Allen Case (Clay McCord), to carry the bulk of the action. McCord gave it his best shot, but the public wanted Fonda, and by season number two had forced him to frequent his series at least every other week. Less dependent on stars than on visuals was "Laramie," a veritable epic of the genre with a huge cast and impressive scope. Slim Sherman (John Smith), Jonesy (Hoagy Carmichael), and Jess Harper (Robert Fuller) were the owners-operators of a ranch and stagecoach station near Laramie, Wyoming. Nothing very profound ever happened, but the show was always busy, laden with action and interesting character players. "The Rebel," on the other hand, was a more solemn and cerebral effort, as Civil War veteran Johnny Yuma (Nick Adams)—who took the South's bitter defeat to heart—roamed the West in search of inner peace. Actually, while this may sound very melodramatic, it

The Cartwright clan of "Bonanza." From left to right: Dan Blocker, Lorne Greene, Pernell Roberts, and Michael Landon.

Leslie Nielson and Jordan "Smokie" Whitfield (right) in "The Swamp Fox." © Walt Disney Productions.

wasn't really. The show never came right out and said, "Yuma is an angry young man *because . . .*"—the way that television had told us that the Lone Ranger upholds justice *because. . . .* But the late Nick Adams was able to suggest these moods without overstating them, creating television's first truly tragic hero. Historically, this is noteworthy because "The Rebel" was the only one of nearly fifty television Westerns to show Reconstruction as a period of hurt and great soul-searching, rather than as a marketplace for the talents of Civil War veterans.

Despite its variable contribution to the series Western in 1959, television also showcased some unusual, alternately crude and florid efforts, programs that spanned from the dim past to the automated future. It's a pity, however, that most of these shows might just as well have been Westerns for all the novelty they brought to the tube. Moving chronologically through the flops, we find Kirk Douglas' Bryna Productions' TV series "Tales of the Vikings," a lavish epic based on Douglas' 1958 film *The*

Vikings. Shot in Europe, the Norse saga featured Jerome Courtland, late of Disney's "Andy Burnett," as a young Viking leader. The adventures were lusty and brawling, and the scope impressive—over a quarter of a million dollars was spent on the costumes alone—but the small picture tube was an insufficient proscenium for the series' grandeur. In this respect, "Riverboat" was more ideally suited to television, since the setting was the relatively restricted confines of the 1840s Mississippi riverboat *Enterprise*. Darren McGavin starred as Capt. Grey Holden, and Burt Reynolds was featured as his pilot, Ben Fraser. Meanwhile, the Klondike was the site of television's 1890s gold-rush epic "The Alaskans," as with old "Sgt. Preston" plots in-hand, sourdoughs Reno McKee (Jeff York, who played Mike Fink in Disney's "Davy Crockett" series) and Silky Harris (Roger Moore) went traipsing about the snows of Northwest Canada. Dorothy Provine costarred as Rocky, a saloon singer. Producers had no better luck with the twentieth century, as Keenan Wynn and Olympic decathalon winner Bob Mathias played "The Troubleshooters," construction supervisors who traveled about the world on jobs. Each week, the men faced a new and colorful diaster, such as a cave-in in Alaska, the transport of equipment through the mountains of Venezuela, and so forth. Less ambitious was "Cannonball," with Paul Birch and William Campbell as Mike and Jerry, the owners of a small trucking service that ran between the United States and Canada. The muscle and drive of these various programs notwithstanding, they failed to attract an audience because their stars were unable to compete with the action and simplicity of the scripts. Then again there are actors who can captivate the public with their voice, manner, or appearance, despite the vehicle, which is precisely what kept James Michener's "Adventures in Paradise" afloat where the others floundered.

On "Adventures in Paradise," acting newcomer Gardner McKay played Adam Troy, a young and active man who sailed the Pacific on his schooner *Tiki*. Seldom had television seen the likes of McKay, a 6′5″ ex-model who simply could not photograph badly. Three thousand fan letters a week were not uncommon for the star, but the quiet, soft-spoken McKay *was* beset by one major problem: the critics all agreed that he was the least talented actor in television history. Even worse than poor reviews, however, was the fact that these comments were couched in terms that were unusually sadistic, even for critics. This writer will not heap injustices on McKay, for he was never given a chance to learn his trade. The producers cast him for his looks, handed him a script, thrust him before a camera, and told him to act. The worse that can be said of McKay is that he tried, in spite of the awful writing that hounded the show. "There were so many characters in every script," McKay once complained, "that there wasn't time for them to do anything but say hello, get arrested, and say goodbye." However, sailing from island to island caused McKay to grow philosophical about it all: "Hollywood is a state of mind that has to be corrected if any measure of contentment is to be achieved. But I have to keep at acting. I have to gain back the respect I lost." There's the hero; not Troy.

Rounding out the 1959 season were two looks at the future. In the more popular series, William Lundigan starred as Col. Edward McCauley of the United States Air Force, one of the "Men In Space." The Colonel was a potent public-relations tool for our fledgling space program, defending it with such gung-ho remarks as "You gotta climb mountains; these are just a few hundred thousand miles higher." Luckily, most of the show's fans were unaware of the fact that the enthusiasm shown on screen was only skin-deep. For, as the forty-five-year-old Lundigan admitted off camera, "I don't know a logarithm from a rocket sled. It's all I can do to drive a

Gardner McKay of "Adventures in Paradise" pilots the Tiki *to new adventures.*

car." In any case, unlike previous space adventures, "Men in Space" was as scientifically accurate as technology would allow. Wisely, however, and to offset the documentary feel of the program, the producers found drama in such extraterrestrial hazards as the spacesuit of an astronaut becoming caught between two sections of a newly assembled space station, McCauley going EVA and drifting away from his spacecraft, and so on. Unfortunately, the Colonel himself took a back seat to the special effects and, like the characters in "The Vikings," "The Alaskans," et al, was never able to develop beyond the "Capt. Video" stage. In this respect, "Man and the Challenge" offered a more interesting hero in Glenn Barton (George Nader) and his men, guinea pigs all in a government-sponsored project to find the limits of human endurance. Barton, an ex-athlete and Marine-turned-researcher, excluded all but the physical from his lexicon. And while critics called both him and this Ivan Tors production sadistic, Barton was one of the few truly unique television heroes. His was a world of muscle rather than moral. If it were cold to the touch, it was at least a break from the domination of the loftier-than-thou hero.

These two men, McCauley and Barton, were accurate reflections of the men who would one day walk on the moon. Yet, while their real-life counterparts—men like Neil Armstrong and Pete Conrad—would be considered heroes, these same characters seemed dull on television. Let the social historians make of that what they will!

5

Camelot and the Hero

"If you happen to be lucky enough to be neurotic, and can go to pieces on the spur of the moment, and then pick yourself back up and do it four more times, then you should make a fairly good television actor."
—George C. Scott
Star of "East Side/West Side"

A brief period of American history known as "The Kennedy Era" bridged the first three years of the sixties, a link between an age of innocence—some would say naiveté—and a cultural renaissance. Television, of course, played an important part in helping to make John F. Kennedy president, four televised debates with then Vice-President Richard Nixon creating a hero of the charismatic senator from Massachusetts. Not surprisingly, the television hero found this a difficult period. The Westerns faded, cop shows were unusually weak, and the name of the game was *novelty*. And novelty there was, in terms of new framing stories and situations. But few programers thought to change the years-old stereotype of the hero himself—that incomplex figure of ever-righteous action. Shows like "The Californians," "The Rebel," "Maverick," and even "Bonanza" had taken steps in this direction, but they were tenuous and isolated steps. The other so-called "human" heroes, like Earl Holliman's Sundance from "Hotel de Paree" or Johnny Staccato were no more realistic than their "Hopalong Cassidy"-era antecedents. Television had not yet learned that it takes more than just hints of greed,

joy, or sadness to create a human character. And Kennedy, who sought to fill the nation with a youthful and patriotic fevor, unwittingly made the Olympian image even more desirable. It was only after his assassination that television and the public began to change their views. The so-called counterculture helped to foster a new breed of American and thereby gave the country a new breed of hero. This is not to say that the classic hero was gone. However, toward the middle of the decade, viewers would see to it that a hero stood or fell on an actor's portrayal, rather than on the character's moral values or altruism.

For one reason or another, a number of promising shows never made it to the home screen in 1960. This is not to say that they were any deeper than their predecessors of the series that did sell. But they were entertaining beyond the norm. These pilots included "Superboy," featuring young Johnny Rockwell as the teenaged Superman; "The Magic of Sinbad," with Lassie's ex-master Tommy Rettig as the Arabian Nights hero; Blake Edwards' sleuthing dandy "Boston Terrier," starring Robert Vaughn; "The Barbarians," with Jack Palance as Rivak of the Punic Wars; a new verson of "Tightrope" known as "Tangier," starring Mike Connors; Jose Ferrer as Agatha Christie's "Hercule Poirot"; and "Lafitte the Pirate," with Fernando Lamas. Clearly, the emphasis was on genres and properties that had not yet been overexposed by television. However, the fact that these shows didn't sell is also indicative of the paradox that programers were simply afraid to break with the fare that had sold the year before.

What did sell in 1960? Well, there were seven Westerns, for starters, the least distinctive of which were "Luke and the Tenderfoot," starring Edgar Buchanan and Carleton Carpenter; Brian Keith as a rootless, pessimistic cowpoke known as "The Westerner"; "Stagecoach West," a reworking of "Overland Trail," with Wayne Rogers as Master Whip Luke Perry, Robert Bray as his corider Simon Kane, and Richard Eyer as Bray's young son David; "The Tall Man," the chronicle of Billy the Kid (Clu Gulager) versus Deputy Sheriff Pat Garrett (Barry Sullivan), whose motto was "My business is the law and I mean to mind it"; and Charles Bateman as both a gunfighter and his twin brother in "Two Faces West." All of these series were gone before season's end, as were the highly touted but barren Westerns "Tate" and Walt Disney's "Daniel Boone."

Tate was an unusual character—a one-armed gunman. Played by David McLean he was, according to press releases,

representative of post Civil War society. His wife and child were killed during the War. Almost simultaneously, Tate's left arm was all but blown from his body at Vicksburg. This left his limb useless. Then he returned home and found his wife and child buried. Any other man might have taken a lawless path, but Tate couldn't. His unyielding conscience structure allowed him no path but bitter righteousness. He is wandering through the West, vainly searching for something to relieve and replace the anguish of his wife's death, and his physical scourge.

Not that his handicap made Tate less than an expert shot. And, just as naturally, the marksman was constantly being pressed to prove his reputation. The only problem with this show was that beyond the grim gimmick of his affliction, Tate was nothing more than a poor man's Johnny Yuma. This same stumbling block was suffered by Disney's "Daniel Boone," which featured Dewey Martin in the title role and appeared on four hour-long segments of "Walt Disney Presents." The rugged pioneer was simply Davy Crockett run once more through the mill. Even Disney was aware of its familiarity. "I don't expect *Boone* to be the hit that *Davy Crockett* was," the filmmaker noted before the first broadcast. "Actually, we had both *Boone* and *Crockett* on our list six years ago and we went with *Crockett*. I don't know how the decision was made. Maybe we flipped a coin."

While we're on the subject of rehashes, several running hits were mimicked in the 1960 season. Lloyd Bridges was joined in "Sea Hunt's" briny waters by "Devlin of the Deep," an Ivan Tors production starring Keith Larsen as Drake Andrews, and Jeremy Slate as

Ron Ely (left) and Jeremy Slate go hunting for a sunken ship in the "Secret of Half Moon Key" episode of "The Aquanauts."

Larry Lahr, free-lance divers of a more sophisticated nature than the chest-pounding Bridges. Unfortunately, Larsen was forced to hang up his flippers after the first season due to a sinus operation that made him, as he put it, "bleed like a sieve when I went down thirty feet." Thus, Ron Ely took over the role and the series became "The Aquanauts." Incidentally, Ely, who would eventually play "Tarzan" on television, had been scheduled to join Gardner McKay on "Adventures in Paradise," to help carry the burden of the show. When Ely became one of "The Aquanauts," his place on the *Tiki* was taken by Guy Stockwell. Also along subsea lines was "Assignment Underwater," with Bill Williams (Kit Carson) as an ex-Marine who became a diver-for-hire.

Elsewhere, "Sgt. Preston" found his old plots being dusted off for a second time and used in "The Royal Canadian Mounted Police," a filmed-on-location series starring Giles Pelletier, John Perkins, and Don Francks as a three-man mounted detachment. Even the disastrous "Alaskans" was "revived" in "Klondike," starring Ralph Taeger as a gold-rush womanizer and adventurer Jeff Durain. However, the most substantial marketplace for clichés this season was in the detective field. Indicative of Hollywood's short-sightedness is the fact that one producer even tried to remake the antiquated "Treasury Men in Action," with Richard Arlen topcast. Fortunately, he got no further than a pilot. But a dozen other entries did make it into the prime-time schedule, despite very little innovation on the part of producers.

"Checkmate" was easily the most interesting of these shows because of its somewhat novel premise: Checkmate, Inc. tried to stop crimes *before* they occurred. The Checkmate team consisted of leader Don Corey (Anthony George), Jed Sills (Doug McClure); and criminology professor Carl Hyatt (Sebastian Cabot). Once again, however, the most interesting conflicts were those that occurred off camera. Anthony George, an intense and dedicated actor, found himself "trapped" by Cabot and McClure, or "The Beard" and "The Smile" as he called them. George felt that he could not compete with the cuddly father figure presented by Cabot, or McClure's sparkling image of youth, and became greatly depressed by the situation. Fortunately, Cary Grant caught up with him one day in the studio commissary. Grant had just seen George perform and sensed right away what his problem was. He advised the novice to "say your lines and be what you are," and forget about the images of the players surrounding him. George did this and quickly found that "I learned to play *off* what they did." The confidence he gained bolstered his performance, and George was able to lick his problem. However, he was not alone in this struggle for identity, particularly where players like "The Smile" were concerned. When the contemporary, style-conscious Kookie of "77 Sunset Strip" became the rage of teenage girls, producers tried to get a regular Kookie-character into every evening program. Thus, for lack of a better phrase, these years between 1958 and 1963 might properly be subtitled "The Era of the Pretty Boys," what with actors such as McClure, Ed Byrnes, and, upcoming, Troy Donahue, George Maharis, Richard Chamberlain, and James Franciscus dominating the airwaves.

Of course teenagers, as a rule, did not watch television late in prime time or on Friday and Saturday evenings. Thus, for their parents, programers came up with detectives who were more mature then Byrnes and Company—men like Rod Taylor, Howard Duff, and Richard Denning. Taylor, fresh from his starring role in George Pal's top-grossing motion picture *The Time Machine*, became Glenn Evans of "Hong Kong," an agent who put a stop to such illicit activities as smuggling, hashish rings, and anti-West saboteurs in the Orient. Duff had the lead in "Dante" as Willie Dante, the tuxedoed owner of the posh *Dante's Inferno* nightclub. As in both "Peter Gunn" and "Staccato," underworld figures

had a way of congregating in Willie's eatery. Lastly, Denning returned to TV in his first series since "Mr. and Mrs. North" as "Michael Shayne," author Brett Halliday's two-fisted, cognac-drinking Irishman, working as a Miami Beach private eye. Each of these men was young enough to grab male viewers with requisite fits of action; handsome enough to hold the ladies; but carefully delineated as worldly wise and not to be mistaken for a fashionably flip and irresponsible "teenage" investigator. Thus, television had heroes enough to please everyone. What they didn't have, as yet, was that blast of originality. If we look back some ten years, we find that "Dante" was an update of "Foreign Assignment," "Hong Kong" was Dan Duryea's "Affairs of China Smith" with a new coat of paint, and "Michael Shayne" was not unlike "Martin Kane." And the facsimiles didn't end here. In fact, these were some of the more enjoyable and smartly mounted series! Less outstanding were "Acapulco," with Robert Taeger and James Coburn as Patrick Malone and Gregg Miles, Korean War veterans turned crime-busting beachcombers in Southern Mexico, ably assisted by Telly Savalas as Carver, a retired criminal lawyer; Richard Wyler as "The Man from Interpol"; "Johnny Midnight," starring Edmund O'Brien as the owner of the Midnight Theatre, where the arts took on a deadly turn: a producer haunted an actor whom he believed was out to kill him, a star became the murderous part he was playing, a ventriloquist's dummy was the only clue to a killing, and so forth; "Dan Raven," featuring Skip Homeier as a man from the Sunset Strip sheriff's office and whom, the actor felt, was simply "a straight man carrying the exposition and feeding the good scenes to the guest stars"; Steve Dunne and Mark Roberts as private eyes Mike and Bob, "The Brothers Brannagen," who operated from the poolside of an Arizona resort; "Dangerous Robin," starring Rich Jason and Jean Blake as globe-trotting insurance investigators; and Arthur Fleming as the "International Detective."

On the periphery of this detective genre, the inevitable "Untouchables" duplicate appeared this season in "The Roaring Twenties," a bird's-eye view of flappers, bathtub gin, and the ever-present speakeasies. Donald May and Rex Reason portrayed newspapermen Pat Garrison and Scott Norris, crusading journalists who covered the underworld. This beat offered ample opportunity for "Untouchables"-like violence, tough mob leaders, hit men, and related period pieces, of which the real show-stopper was former "Alaskans" costar Dorothy Provine as Charleston Club entertainer Pinky Pinkham. Actually, Miss Provine's song-and-dance routines did more to evoke the Prohibition Era

George Maharis with guest star Julie Newmar in an episode of "Route 66."

than any of the series' other elements. Unlike "The Untouchables," "The Roaring Twenties" didn't acknowledge the existence of a world outside the liquor dens. This made for a bland series that an occasional reference to sports, politics, or other topical events might have helped. Another dry pastiche was "The Islanders," a cross between "Sky King" and "Adventures in Paradise," as airplane pilots James Philbrook and William Reynolds scoured the Pacific for thrills and money. Of course, the artistic and commercial failure of these two series did not mean that a hybrid effort couldn't be well done. For instance, "Route 66" was a perfect example of a successfully recycled old theme—that of men leaving their home in search of their souls. Fortunately, creator Stirling Silliphant had the courage to bring this traditionally Western theme to the present, spicing it with unusual taste and sensitivity.

"Route 66" starred Martin Milner as Tod Stiles, the son of a millionaire, and George Maharis as Buzz Murdock, a poor boy from New York's Hell's Kitchen who used to work for Tod's father. When the elder Stiles died, he left neither boy any money, so they decided to drive cross-country looking for work and adventure. With a different setting and changing local values in every episode, the boys usually found both—and more. Once again there was conflict on the set as the brooding Maharis couldn't stand his sunny companion. Silliphant

defined their personalities and the problem both: "The teenagers are crazy about Maharis, but he bores their parents stiff. He's too primitive. The adults like Marty because he's a gentleman. They only tolerate George because Marty seems to like him." To Maharis, however, the personality clash went deeper than what the public saw on "Route 66." "We have nothing in common," he once glowered about Milner. "He's basically a snob and looks down on everybody." Milner's retort: "He sounds like he's kind of mad at me. I'm sorry." As one might imagine, this tension led to the point where Maharis felt he had no recourse but to leave the show. He was replaced by Glen Corbett as Lincoln Case, a man who might have been Maharis' twin save for his more tolerant disposition. Returning to Stiles' white convertible, the men drove on to new adventures.

Beyond the foundation of *concept*, perhaps the most crucial element of a series is casting. To this end, shows have sometimes built their frameworks around an actor's own persona or image. Two such programs premiered in 1960, the finer effort being "The Law and Mr. Jones," starring James Whitmore as attorney Abraham Lincoln Jones. Jones was a scrappy fighter for justice who involved himself with clients regardless of the fee they could pay or the size of the case. Operating from a converted brownstone in "a large Eastern city," Jones was a lawyer who tempered principle with a piercing insight into human failings, a union with which viewers were unable to identify. This is not to imply that a series must exhibit civic responsibility to be good: "The Third Man," based on the 1950 Carol Reed film, gave Orson Welles' role of Harry Lime to Michael Rennie, who turned the one-time man of mystery into a suave financial speculator who doubled as an amateur sleuth. And it was Rennie's show all the way. According to the late actor, a man for whom the word class was invented, "Justice is Harry Lime's major concern. He's a man who likes to feel the adrenalin work, who gets his kicks out of danger." Unfortunately, audiences found Lime's drive and continental values just a bit too elusive for their tastes. However, viewers also sent a trio of lackluster entries back to the locker room: "African Patrol," with John Bentley; "The Blue Angels," an Air Force adventure starring Dennis Cross, Warner Jones, Michael Galloway, and Don Gordon; and "National Velvet," based on the 1944 film and the worst horse series ever to reach the home screen. Young Lori Martin saved the featured stallion from the glue factory after it had been caught stealing broccoli, unaware that the producers had a nastier fate of tawdry plots and poor scripting awaiting them both!

Did any of these failures teach Hollywood a lesson? Yes and no. *Yes* because programers returned to the ratings war in 1961 with some excellent new series. *No* because the tripe still outnumbered the gems by a hefty margin. First, the positive side of things. Network executives exhibited rare perception by not going with such routine Western pilots as Kirk Douglas' "Indian Fighter" and the Chad Everett-Evan McCord vehicle "Tumbleweed." Instead, they managed to work a miracle or two with some cop and lawyer shows, not to mention a pair of doctor programs that struck ratings gold. The medics were Ben Casey and Dr. Kildare, and they both set up a long and healthy practice in the top ten sector of A. C. Nielsen's popularity charts. Casey (Vincent Edwards) was the Chief Resident in Neurosurgery at Country General Hospital, a brawny, scowling man famous for fighting with every character in the script and every person on the set. Kildare (Richard Chamberlain) was quite the opposite—a baby-faced and painfully naive intern at Blair General Hospital, who waited three seasons just to get his residency!

In terms of audience affection, the young physicians drew a decidedly different crowd. Casey had an edge with the adults, since he was both introspective and confident; Kildare was simply a clean and wholesome

Vincent Edwards as Ben Casey.

human being, and the ideal of teenage girls everywhere. However, both men were skilled technicians who saved lives and always acted in a patient's best interests—something that automatically qualified them for the mantle of hero. Yet, they were also filled with the impulsive vigor of youth and thus required constant steadying by an external conscience. Casey's mentor was Dr. Zorba (Sam Jaffe), a wizened, wispy-voice influence, while Kildare's Dr. Gillespie (Raymond Massey) was a soured and sterner critic. In each case, however, here was something unique to television: a return to the ancient Greek concept of the hero, a brave and virtuous man, but one who still needed gods and oracles to counsel his journey through life. The only twist was that in "Dr. Kildare" and "Ben Casey" when mistakes were made it was usually "gods" Gillespie and Zorba who made them! The hero was still beyond mortal corruption! Thus, it was with considerable pleasure that a small but devout slice of the viewing public welcomed "The Defenders" to television.

Few shows have been as honored by critics as "The Defenders." Part of this praise was due to the fact that father and son lawyers Lawrence and Ken Preston (E. G. Marshall and Robert Reed) lost as many cases as they won. However, it was also inspired by uncompromising stories with enough guts to reverse the standard courtroom formulae. For instance, seldom did a guilty party fall to pieces in the last reel and confess to a crime. More often than not, wrongdoers were presented as attractive, sometimes very pleasant, characters who either felt that they had done nothing wrong, or honestly could not help what they had done. Meanwhile, the victims themselves often lacked any virtue whatsoever. This was not to be construed as an attempt to laud criminal behavior. But it did convey the message that sometimes guilt and innocence are not as cut and dried as "Perry Mason" would have had us believe. A case in point: How would the reader have judged a man who, in the segment called "Kill or Be Killed," was wrongly charged with a crime and, frightened, murdered a guard at Sing Sing in order to escape a death penalty, unaware that the court had just reversed its original decision and found him innocent of the first crime? Clearly, "The Defenders" was not intended to be a leisurely hour of entertainment—something that did not help it win a large following. Too, the Prestons were not run-of-the-mill TV supermen. Lawrence was an overly emotional man; his son was a dry, oftentimes dull novice to the bar. Compared to what we have seen thus far, this hardly makes them television's most dynamic heroes. However, as with Abraham Lincoln Jones, the Prestons were

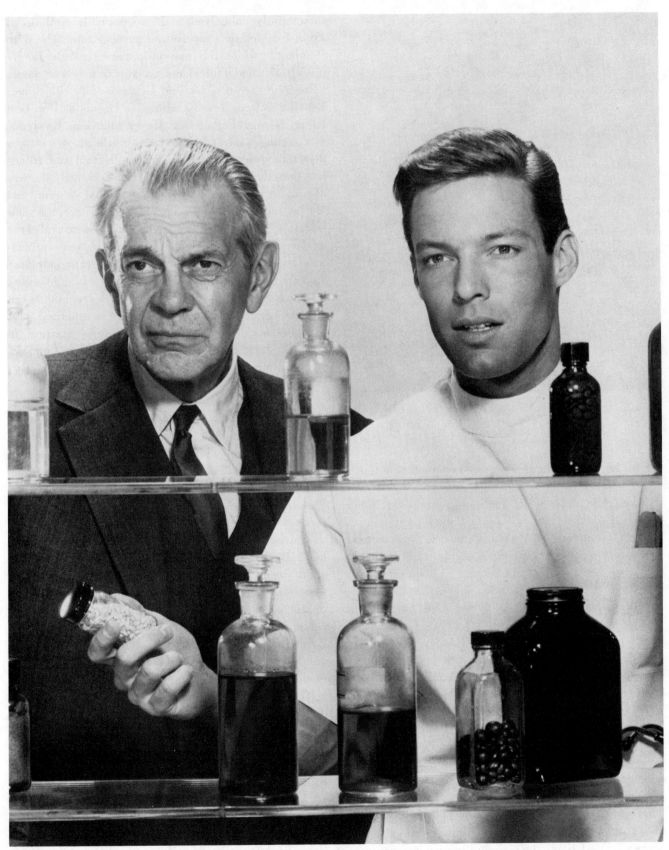

Raymond Massey and Richard Chamberlain of "Dr. Kildare."

Mark Richman as Nicholas Cain in "Cain's Hundred."

soulful heroes, among the first such characters to find a spot on television.

Like "The Defenders," there were numerous other efforts staged creatively within the limited perimeters of genre programming. Particularly unusual were some of this season's police shows. For example, capitulating to the latest tools at the crime-busters' disposal was a branch of the police department known as "The New Breed," Leslie Nielsen, John Beradine, and Byron Morrow were Lt. Price Adams, Sgt. Vince Cavelli, and Capt. Keith Gregory of the elite Los Angeles Metro Squad, who captured lawbreakers with computers, heat detectors, and other electronic gadgetry. However, in another part of town, one Nicholas Cain (Mark Richman) went about his antiunderworld activities in a less sophisticated but no less effective manner. A shady syndicate lawyer, he finally answered the call of his conscience and turned against the mob figures he once defended. "I don't want to keep looking for legal loopholes," he told an associate in the first episode. "I don't want to keep giving advice on how to stay out of jail." And his vow was to put one hundred underworld figures behind bars, thus accounting for the program title of "Cain's Hundred."

Two new series that had roots in other media were also

thoughtfully conceived and exceptionally well done. From Ed McBain's top-selling novels came "The 87th Precinct," while the motion picture *Asphalt Jungle* (1950) spawned a television program of the same name. "The 87th Precinct" boasted a superb cast, with Robert Lansing as Det. Steve Carella, Ron Harper as Det. Bert Kling, Norman Fell as Det. Meyer, and Gena Rowlands as Carella's wife Teddy. Lansing made his detective a determined man who was more intellectual and articulate than the average television cop. Contrarily, he was also more sensitive. Fell was the cynical veteran, and Harper the young, impetuous rookie. However, the show had its greatest impact in Miss Rowlands' portrayal of the deaf-mute Teddy. Indeed, her very warm, very optimistic scenes had a way of obfuscating whatever minor flaws appeared in plot or production. "Asphalt Jungle" didn't have this pathos. It was harder and more cruel than even "Naked City," although both new series inherited their predecessor's stark New York locales. Starring in "Asphalt Jungle" were Jack Warden as Police Commissioner Mathew Gower, Arch Johnson as Capt. Gus Honochek, and Bill Smith as Sgt. Danny Keller.

Only three Western shows premiered in 1961, something of a drought when we consider what has gone before. The most colorful of these was "Frontier Circus," the adventures of a touring big top in the 1880s. Chill Wills starred as owner Col. Casey Thompson, John Derek was featured as his assistant, Ben Travis, and Richard Jaekel appeared as Tom Gentry, the carnival scout. "Whispering Smith" was slightly less extravagant, the story of Police Chief Smith (Audie Murphy) who, with his right-hand man, Det. Romack (Guy Mitchell), maintained the peace in Denver of the 1870s. Finally, there was "The Gunslinger," a Charles Marquis Warren production starring Tony Young as Cord, an undercover agent for Cavalry Captain Zachary Wingate (Preston Foster) in the post-Civil War frontier. Of these series, only "Frontier Circus" managed to squeeze out a respectable run.

The non-Western properties that exhibited varying displays of originality or plagiarism were "Sir Francis Drake," an oceangoing Lancelot—famous for defeating the Spanish Armada in 1588—with Terrence Morgan as the English naval hero and Jean Kent as Queen Elizabeth; Cameron Mitchell as ex-ad-agency executive Lackland, who threw away his career to become the South Pacific's troubleshooting "Beachcomber"; and, also haunting the tropical climes, Ben Gregory (Barry Coe), Paul Templin (Bret Halsey) and Eric Jason (Gary Lockwood) as Hawaiian-based magazine writers in "Follow the Sun." Broderick Crawford was a dock detective in "King of Diamonds," his principal adversaries being smugglers; George Nader was "Shannon," an insurance investigator specializing in the transportation field; James Franciscus and James Philbrook were also insurance investigators, located in New York as "The Investigators"; and Stephen McNally was Paul Marino who, in "Target: The Corruptors," used his newspaper column to expose rackets that hit the little fellow or drained the public pocketbook, such as phony charities, corrupt unions, etc. There were even plans to air yet *another* version of "Tightrope," called "The Expendables," but it did not survive past the pilot stage. Other cloak-and-dagger test shows that failed to make the grade were "Pentagon," "Attorney General," "Las Vegas Beat"—with Peter Graves as a press agent—Rory Calhoun's "Caribbean," "Small Town D.A.," and "Lanny Budd: Presidential Agent."

The remaining heroes of 1961 appeared in the action programs "Ripcord," "Straightaway," and "Danger Man." The first two efforts were average potboilers framed with ornaments never before seen in a regular TV series. As its name implies, "Ripcord" was about skydivers—in this case, free-lance parachutists Ted McKeever (Larry Pennell) and Jim Buckley (Ken Curtis, who joined the cast of "Gunsmoke" in 1964 as the crusty Festus Haggen). According to press releases the diving duo came "Zooming out of the skies! A new breed of hero and man's most incredible experience: human flight without wings!" In terms of drama, this meant absolutely nothing except that the heroes could now engage in fisticuffs while in free-fall rather than on boring old terra firma. "Straightaway" also gave its characters the new battleground of a racetrack. Scott Ross (Brian Kelly) and Clipper Hamilton (John Ashley) ran the Straightaway Garage, where they built race cars, struggled with crooked drivers, overcame sabotaged vehicles, and survived a number of grudge matches.[21] However, in "Danger Man" there was more than just flavor. There was quality, as well as a glimpse of television as it would be a few years later. Produced in Great Britain, "Danger Man" was shown in the United States as "Secret Agent," with the always excellent Patrick McGoohan as the two-fisted, tongue-in-cheek adversary of freedom's enemies, John Drake of British Intelligence. Although this wasn't the first spy series to appear on television, it was an advance scout for genre boom that would affect both film and TV. Drake appeared on the scene just months before the release of the first James Bond film, *Dr. No* (1962), and was caught in the wake of the subsequent craze. Remarkably, it would take only two seasons for Hollywood to be convinced that the genre was

safe enough for the investment of American dollars.

As far as television heroes were concerned, 1962 was an enigma. There were only eleven new shows pertinent to our study, as situation comedies such as "The Beverly Hillbillies" and "McHale's Navy" joined holdovers from previous seasons to rule the ratings roost. Yet, nearly half of the new home-screen heroes managed to attract a formidable share of the audience: two Westerns, a pair of medical shows, and a program about war.

The World War II series "Combat" was among the finest series that television has ever produced. Vic Morrow and Rick Jason starred as Sgt. Chip Saunders and Lt. Gil Hanley, who led their men throughout Europe after the D-Day landing at Normandy Beach. Pierre Jalbert was featured as Caje. Although there was action aplenty, "Combat" did not glorify war. Long before it became fashionable, the producers were decrying the childish politics and waste that are both the cause and by-products of war. Perhaps this was best illustrated by one episode in which Saunders and a fellow sergeant (Albert Salmi) were ordered to go behind enemy lines and reconnoiter for an important battle. The necessary information was secured at the cost of Salmi's life. Presenting himself to Hanley, Saunders then learned that the battle plans were changed shortly after

Vic Morrow of "Combat."

Zina Bethune and Shirl Conway were "The Nurses"; when their series failed to raise the anticipated audience, Dr. Tazinski (Michael Tolan) and Dr. Steffan (Joseph Campanella) joined the cast, and the show became "The Doctors and the Nurses."

their departure, and that his report was useless.

Morrow and Jason were the perfect spokesmen for the pain and business ends of war, respectively. Morrow was a dour, Brando-esque actor who literally threw himself into the role. He gave the battle-weary Saunders just the right dash of causticity to move his viewers. Jason was his opposite: a man who liked being a star as much as he enjoyed acting. Accordingly, Jason had no trouble presenting Hanley as a more superficial, by-the-book soldier than the sergeant. That these characters were responsible for "Combat's" appeal can be seen in the failure of that season's second war program, "The Gallant Men." Like "Combat," "The Gallant Men" had a resident cynic in the Ernie Pyle-like war correspondent Conley Wright (Robert McQueeny), who covered the exploits of Capt. Benedict (William Reynolds) and his dogfaces in Italy. The twist here was Benedict, quick to send his men into battle, was less than anxious to taste of war himself. Perhaps this touch of cowardice in the leader of "The Gallant Men" turned viewers away. As sick of battle as Saunders and Hanley may have been, they were never backward in risking their lives for men or a cause.

On the medical front, as one might have expected, the Casey-Kildare inertia helped sweep "The Nurses" to an admirable position on the Nielsen chart. Significantly, however, the show did not achieve anywhere near the success of its predecessors. The reason for this, alas, was that "The Nurses" didn't feature a sexy male figure over whom the ladies could swoon. Alden General Hospital's one prominent male was Dr. Kiley (Edward Binns), and he was more a Zorba figure than a strapping and energetic Vincent Edwards. This left the domineering veteran nurse Liz Thorpe (Shirl Conway) and novice Gail Lucas (Zina Bethune) to carry the show. Dramatically, the girls did a fine job. It was in clearing the hurdle that separates a modest success from a strong success that their impetus fell short. In this respect, "The Eleventh Hour" was a more commercial show. The leads were forensic psychiatrist Dr. Theodore Bassett (Wendell Corey), the guardian figure, and his young partner, Dr. Paul Graham (Jack Ging). Beyond the generic public interest in any look at psychiatry, the program occasionally linked up with Dr. Kildare so that a story beginning on one would end on the other. Since "The Eleventh Hour" was aimed at a generally more sophisticated audience, this interplay helped both series.

Shading from legalistic medicine to legalistic crusaders, we find the old rebel Nick Adams on another soul-searching venture—this one through the streets of Manhattan in "Saints and Sinners." Adams portrayed newspaperman Nick Alexander of the fictitious *New York Bulletin*, with John Larkin as his editor, Mark Grainger, and Richard Erdman as Klugie, a staff photographer. Alexander was a typically headstrong reporter who disobeyed Grainger's orders, got himself into trouble, but always came out of it with a scoop. As the editor was moved to comment at the conclusion of nearly every episode, "I ought to fire you for gross insubordination . . . and journalistic enterprise!" "Saints and Sinners," however, was fired by the network as were this season's other three metropolitan efforts.

Originally announced as "333 Montgomery"—a la "77 Sunset Strip"—"Sam Benedict" starred Edmund O'Brien in a dramatization of San Francisco trial lawyer Jack Ehrlich's career. There was nothing extraordinary here, save for O'Brien's ability to change, in a moment, from a dazzling figure of efficiency to a paternal man, ready to counsel a client on life, liberty, or the pursuit of a witness. "Mr. Smith Goes to Washington" also spotlighted a father-figure in Fess Parker, who re-created the famous James Stewart role as idealistic freshman senator Eugene Smith for this short-lived series. Prior to this, Parker had done an unsold pilot for a Western called "The Code of Jonathan West." Finally, Lloyd Bridges found that, like Parker, he too had fared better in his first stab at television than in "The Lloyd Bridges Show." Bridges played journalist Adam Shepherd, with the gimmick that he literally became the person whose adventure he was covering. By midseason this format was discarded, and Bridges sat out the series' run by serving as its host.

Of the four new Westerns, two were about the modern-day rodeo, and these were the two that failed to make the ratings grade. "The Wide Country" was Earl Holliman's second unsuccessful series, the story of a man's relationship with his younger brother, set against a broncobusting background. Mitch Guthrie (Holliman) was a champion rider who nonetheless believed himself to be a "rodeo bum," and insisted that his young brother Andy (Andrew Prine) go to college and make something of his life. Naturally, Andy wanted only to be like Mitch, and therein lay the rub. However, this quarreling over Andy's future was an ultimately repetitious distraction from the more entertaining world of the rodeo. For this reason, "Stoney Burke" was a better, albeit less personal, show, its sole concentration being on the hard life of a rodeo performer. Jack Lord played Burke, an independent star with a traveling show. Up-and-coming actors Warren Oates and Bruce Dern portrayed his

associates, sweaty parasites who offered an interesting change of pace from the noble Jay Silverheels-Andy Devine breed of sidekick. Of historic value, however, was not "Stoney Burke," per se, but what it almost inspired among the programming ranks. Early in the season, when it looked as if this hard-hitting "man's" show were going to catch on, scripts were written for a total of four spinoff programs. These were tentatively titled "Kincaid," "Border Town," "Mr. Kingston," and "Tack Reynolds," based on characters or locales in the show. While none of these projects was ever filmed, it proves that the "spinoff phenomenon," currently a television vogue, is not unique to the 1970s.

The pair of Westerns that did manage to capture the public's fancy for several reasons were "The Virginian" and "Empire." "The Virginian" was television's first weekly "movie," each program running a full ninety minutes. Based on Owen Wister's 1901 novel, the stories centered around the Shiloh Ranch, a Wyoming Territory spread owned by Judge Henry Garth (Lee J. Cobb). James Drury portrayed the title character, Garth's stern, silent foreman. Doug McClure was the irresponsible and wild Trampas, Pippa Scott played newspaper owner Molly Wood, Gary Clarke appeared as the Virginian's best friend, Steve, and Roberta Shore was seen as Garth's daughter Betsy. The theme of the show, set in the 1880s, was that a century-old way of life known as the West was fast being destroyed by progress from the East. This, of course, was not a change that well suited the old-time pioneers and rough-hewn men of the prairie, and "The Virginian" accurately contrasted these conflicting cultures. Only the Virginian himself, heroic in body and spirit, refused to be broken or moved by this clash of two realities. In fact, Drury was actually playing an antihero, a man more interested in his world than the world around him. In 1970, the series became "The Men From Shiloh," was advanced to 1890 and added Lee Majors and Stuart Whitman to the cast.

"Empire" was of a different orientation entirely. Although it, too, dealt with a huge spread—the half-million-acre Garret Ranch—"Empire" was a soap opera that lacked the inventive focus of "The Virginian." Richard Egan starred as Jim Redigo, foreman of the homestead owned by Lucia Garret (Anne Symour), Connie Garret (Terry Moore), and Tal Garret (Ryan O'Neal). Like Drury, Egan played an iron-willed loner who refused to compromise with his bosses, hired hands, or any outside element that happened along. In fact, Egan was so much more credible and popular than his costars that, by the second season, "Empire" had become "Redigo" and both O'Neal and the ladies were

"The Virginian" crew prepares a scene featuring (from left to right) Hugh O'Brian, Roberta Shore, and James Drury.

gone, replaced by Charles Bronson as Paul, and Warren Vanders as Chuck.

Depending upon one's point of view, news that a program called "Diagnosis: Danger" was being considered for the 1963 season seemed either embarrassing or galling. How could this union of television's two hottest properties miss the mark? Well, for Hollywood, it proved rather mortifying upon reflection, since the proposed series was about a detective-physician. There comes a time when commercialization can be carried too far! Thankfully, upon viewing the test film, Hollywood felt that a limit had been reached and the concept was abandoned. Instead, producers went with undiluted genre pieces for 1963, such as a spy program, three Westerns, one very tame armed-forces entry, three law-enforcement agents, and a sole psychiatrist. Then there were rare or never-before-seen vehicles for heroes

like an attractive circus adventure, two series about English teachers, a bold experiment in which a social worker was the continuing character, the unending story of an escaped convict, and one of the most consistently engrossing programs ever seen on television, a nonfiction anthology series about American history.

Conceived under the title "The Free and the Brave" and filmed as "The Adventurers," the show was finally broadcast as "The Great Adventure." Each week, this immaculately produced, hour-long omnibus told the story of a laudable American figure who was usually—but not always—involved in the event that made him famous. For instance, there were episodes that dealt with the execution of Nathan Hale (Jeremy Slate) and the Underground Railroad activities of Harriet Tubman (Ruby Dee); but there were also shows about Jefferson Davis (Michael Rennie) and his attempt to smuggle the defeated South's remaining wealth to the West, where he intended to begin the Confederacy anew; or, in a lighter vein, how President Grover Cleveland (Leif Ericson) had a minor oral operation performed on board a train to keep the public from hearing of it and becoming unduly alarmed. And if the stories themselves or Van Heflin's heartfelt prologue and epilogue failed to inspire the viewer, then there was always the program's opening music. Against a montage of shining monents in American history, "The Great Adventure" had one of the most stirring title themes oever composed for a television series!

Less kind to our nation's past were "The Dakotas," about U.S. Marshals Del Stark (Chad Everett), J. D. Smith (Jack Elam), Frank Ragan (Larry Ward), and Vance Porter (Michael Greene), and their fight to uphold law and order in the Dakota Territory; "Temple Houston," a Jack Webb Western starring Jeffrey Hunter as Texan Sam Houston's son, a full-blooded frontier lawyer; and "The Travels of Jaimie McPheters," starring Kurt Russell as Jaimie and Dan O'Herlihy as Doc Sardius McPheters, a pair of Kentuckians who joined a Westward trek during the Gold Rush era. Based on Robert Lewis Taylor's Pulitzer Prize-winning novel, the series gave kids an uncommon hero, a gutsy twelve-year-old who learned about life at an early age. However, "Jaimie McPheters," like its companion efforts, were destined to exit by season's end, as was a tenuous plan to introduce Guy Williams in the continuing role of Ben Cartwright's younger brother Will on "Bonanza."

Like the luckless new Westerns, technology made only tentative stabs at television with the unsold pilots "Jet Port," featuring Bill Williams ("Assignment Underwater"), and the X-15 saga, "Project X," starring Michael Rennie. One series that did find a spot for itself in afternoon schedules was the popular new children's show "Fireball XL-5," starring detailed marionettes and excellently scaled sets. Even the minions of contemporary justice found themselves thwarted, as Paul Thompson (Ed Stroll), the "Congressional Investigator," vanished after a short run, and "The Card and the Badge," based on John Creasey's Inspector West stories, never made it beyond the pilot stage. Only "Arrest and Trial" managed to survive for an entire season due to its running time—ninety minutes a week, a length not easily plugged with substitute fare—and the appeal of its actors. Leads Ben Gazarra and Chuck Connors were able to pull a steady crowd despite the dubious merits of their showcase. Gazarra appeared as Los Angeles detective Nick Anderson, who in the first forty-five minutes of each episode tracked down a suspect and put him behind bars. In the "Trial" segment, attorney John Egan (Connors) tried to prove the defendant innocent.

Needless to say, there was no love lost between Anderson and Egan, which made for the series' most interesting moments. But the overall effect of "Arrest and Trial" was that of breathlessness. The show was always racing to touch all of its bases—from crime to enter Anderson to exit Anderson and enter Egan, to verdict to exit Egan—week after week after. With all this plot going on, there was never any room for characterization. And ninety minutes is a long time to sit and watch cardboard cutouts hurry about their business. Still, it was a clever idea that, with a bit more elbow room, might have been a unique saga of the modern judicial process. Thus, we are left with only one hit among this season's crime-busters: Gene Barry's "Burke's Law."

Although the show became "Amos Burke: Secret Agent" in its second season—to capitalize on the James Bond phenomenon—little would change in terms of the character himself. Burke was simply a millionaire who enjoyed intrigue. In "Burke's Law" he was a captain on the Los Angeles police force who traveled around town in a customized Rolls Royce. In "Amos Burke," he undertook clandestine overseas missions for the United States government. In both instances, Barry was surrounded by opulence and stunning women, and always played his character with tongue-in-cheek. "I badly wanted to do comedy," the actor said. "Drama is easy. You do a scene—a woman is going to have a baby and they yell 'Quick, hot water!' and you're involved. But it's difficult to make an audience chuckle." More specifically, Barry called upon his "Bat Masterson" repertoire of glibness and dapper elegance for Burke. "I see *Burke's Law* in terms of the Old World. Amos Burke has this worldliness and sophistication. People ask, 'Why is he a cop?' but hell, he wouldn't be happy sitting in a stock exchange seat! He's alive, vital, now!" It is a character type on which Barry has cornered the television market.

Speaking of character types, a phenomenal television experiment called "East Side/West Side," brought out the fiery, vengeful devil in George Campbell Scott. The tantrum was inspired by the cancellation of a series that stands alone in its downbeat timbre and relevance. Scott, the Oscar-winning star of such films as *Patton* (1968) and *The Hindenburg* (1975), portrayed Manhattan welfare worker Neil Brock in a program that was banned in twenty-six major Southern cities. The reason, according to producer David Susskind, was that "we've had Negro [sic] actors playing doctors, architects, and lawyers." "East Side/West Side" also had plots that were abjectly depressing and a main character who was the antipode of the romantic hero seen in most television fare. "He came, he saw, and he was defeated," one industry observer was moved to write of Brock. Yet, it was all perfectly valid as, to paraphrase Scott, people like Brock can't win, at least not in the beginning. They've got to learn as they mature. And Scott had hoped that the series would survive long enough for this to happen. "Three years from now," he said,

> I don't want to be the same old Matt Dillon shooting the same old six gun at the same old heavy while Chester drags around the same old game leg. I want this character to change organically, professionally, and even physically, if that seems logical. Look at me; I'm not the same person I was three years ago. Everybody else changes; why not a TV character?

Several months later, when the show was dropped due to poor ratings, he was much less pragmatic. "Brock was becoming different," Scott proclaimed angrily in *TV Guide*:

> He began to change some of his ways of speech and of dealing with people, and we made him a congressman's advisor. Ultimately, we would have had him come to a parting of the ways with the congressman, and Brock would have entered the area of active politics himself.

In short, the fate of "East Side/West Side" was that of any TV show in which the hero cannot always rescue his damsels in distress. It's a sad fact of the industry that must be changed. Helping to raise our fallen Quixote each week were Elizabeth Wilson as Frieda Hechlinger, director of the welfare agency, and Cicely Tyson as his secretary, Jane Foster.

If Scott were a hero at his most inglorious, then David Janssen was the supreme TV martyr in "The Fugitive." Had he not been the main character of his own series, Dr. Richard Kimble would have fit neatly into an episode of "The Defenders." Returning home one night, Kimble found his wife murdered and a one-armed man (Bill Raisch) fleeing the scene of the crime.[22] Kimble was found guilty of murder but received a strange reprieve: en route to prison, his train was derailed and Kimble escaped. Throughout the next six years, he roamed from town to town, searching for Raisch and obscurity, with police Lt. Gerard (Barry Morse) always one step behind him. In the last episode, Kimble caught up with the one-armed killer at a carnival and it all ended, if not happily, then neatly. Ironically, according to producer Quinn Martin, the question of whether or not Kimble should have turned himself in was never even broached. The reason? "We've received no complaints," he assured an interviewer, "not even from police departments."

One of the things that helped endear Kimble to the public—beyond Janssen's subtle, male-pleasing virility and lady-killing gentility—was his lack of heroic stature. He was an ordinary guy living in suburbia, a angle with which most viewers could identify. Thus, the show vicariously put "us" in a race for our lives, a pseudomasochistic situation not unlike banging your head against a wall because it feels good when you stop. However, it now becomes clear why Janssen's next job was selling Excedrin in TV commercials.

There are those who claim that acting in general has a bit of this "Fugitive" complex in it, being a frustrating, self-abusive art. Certainly actors Mike Connors and James Franciscus experienced varying degrees of this futility in 1963. Connors made yet another pilot—although this one, at least, was not another remake of "Tightrope." Called "Turning Point," the high-school drama cast the rugged Connors as a somewhat docile school teacher, and it didn't sell. Franciscus, meanwhile, had been offered the role of Dr. Kildare before it was given to his lookalike, Richard Chamberlain. But he couldn't accept the assignment due to the seventeen days remaining in a previous contract. Instead, in one of Fate's ironic twists, he was signed to play a high-school teacher, an English instructor by the name of Mr. Novak, while Connors went back to the proverbial drawing board! Fortunately, "Mr. Novak" was a ratings success, while Connors' smash hit "Mannix" was not far down the road. So, for the actors—like Kimble—everything eventually worked out for the best.

John Novak faced all the problems that one would expect to find in a modern high school, and then some. There were pregnancies among students and pupils headed for juvenile delinquency, but there were also episodes of a more probing nature, involving teacher brutality or such personal stories as Novak's being unable to pay his bills on a teacher's salary. Of course, with Dean Jagger featured as the father-figure principal, Albert Vane—Burgess Meredith would replace him the following year as principal Martin Woodbridge—the show was really "Dr. Kildare" in a secondary school. And where there's smoke there's fire: Jason Evers starred as the early Associate English Professor Joseph Howe, with Henry Jones as the frail and kindly Zorba figure Dean Frederick Baker, when Ben Casey went to college in "Channing." However, the young audience that adored "Mr. Novak" couldn't identify with the college setting of "Channing," and the show was not renewed at season's end. Like the doctors, however, the teachers were both cleancut, faultlessly noble, and never wrong. In a few years they would call this "camp"; in 1963, it was still Camelot.

Rounding out the season were "Espionage," an anthology show that re-created history's greatest spy missions; "The Lieutenant," starring Gary Lockwood as Lt. Rice of Camp Pendleton in a dramatic version of "Gomer Pyle"; "Breaking Point," a psychiatric drama starring Paul Richards as young Dr. McKinely Thompson of a Los Angeles out-patient clinic headed by Eduard Franz as the rabbinical Dr. William Raymer; and, finally, there was "The Greatest Show on Earth," based on the 1953 Cecil B. DeMille circus picture. This last series was conventional of epics in that, despite its various interpersonal involvements, the scenery tended to dominate the players. For this reason, producer Stanley Colbert signed 6'4" Jack Palance to balance the scales as Johnny Slate, a powerful, no-nonsense circus boss. "The circus is larger-than-life," Colbert said, "so you need a larger-than-life lead. However," he added, setting a limit on his commercialism, "I'm also leaving social drama to *The Defenders*, subduodenal ulcers to *Ben Casey*, and deep-rooted psychoses to *The Eleventh Hour*." Which pretty well sums up the heroic vehicle, circa 1963.

6

Holy Parody, Batman!

We've lost the police, Missa Blitt!
—Kato to Britt Reid, alias
"The Green Hornet," in a 1940 comic book

The drama of one generation was about to become the comedy of the next. The nation had seen one of its great heroes murdered in the streets of Dallas, and found itself reexamining its commitment to the ideal of the indestructible hero. The first step in this process was to take another look at the heroes from television's halcyon days. Tickled with the impossible sincerity and invulnerability of such characters as the Lone Ranger and Hopalong Cassidy, people began referring to these saints as *camp*, characters and situations so pretentiously contrived that they could not be taken seriously. But where TV made a killing was not only in reviving and rerunning these old series, but in producing new ones. Thus, from a union of the camp culture and the popularity of the spy genre was born the year's most phenomenally popular program, "The Man from U.N.C.L.E."

"The Man from U.N.C.L.E." was conceived by producer Sam Rolfe and author Ian Fleming. Fleming, the creator of James Bond, liked the idea of doing a tongue-in-cheek Bond, rather than one who was simply facile as in the movies. Fleming came up with a proposal for a series called "Solo," but the name and sketchy outline were his only contributions. A heart attack prevented him from attempting the rigors of a weekly

series. At this point, the Bond filmmakers entered the picture. They owned the rights to any Bond television ventures, and indicated that a minor character in one of Fleming's novels just happened to be called Solo. They asked Rolfe to change the title, which he did—although it wasn't until July of 1964, two months before the show's premiere, that he came up with "The Man from U.N.C.L.E." However, he had grown accustomed to the name of Solo and decided to retain it for his secret agent.

Napoleon Solo (Robert Vaughn, who was fresh from playing Gary Lockwood's superior officer in "The Lieutenant") was Agent Eleven of U.N.C.L.E., a name that Rolfe explained was "a funny one, and kind of provocative. People thought it stood for Uncle Sam, which it didn't. Or the U.N., which it didn't. Finally, so many people wanted to know what the initials stood for, that we had to make up something to fit." The anagram, he decided, represented the United Network Command for Law Enforcement. And while the opponents of democracy took many guises during the series' lengthy run, the most nefarious schemes were usually initiated by *Thrush* which, as Rolfe described it, "was a safety device. If I wanted someone to do something really awful, and I couldn't think of a good motive, I'd say, 'Well, he's doing it for *Thrush*.'" Assisting Solo in most of his escapades was David McCallum as Ilya Kuryakin. Leo G. Carroll costarred as Alexander Waverly, the head of U.N.C.L.E.; the basic premise of the show was that in every episode, an average American citizen would be accidentally but irrevocably swept up in U.N.C.L.E.'s battle against the forces of evil.

Naturally, it would take a season or two for Hollywood to saturate the market with "Man from U.N.C.L.E." imitations, so eight of the ten remaining "hero programs" in 1964 were of a comparatively somber nature. The exceptions were "The Rogues" and Ivan Tors' "Flipper." "Flipper," of course, was the bottle-nosed dolphin who lived in the waters off the Florida Keys and who, weekly, helped marine preserve ranger Porter Ricks (Brian Kelly) out of sundry oceanic scrapes. "The Rogues"— whose motto was "honor before honesty"—were no less slippery than "Flipper," a group of high-class chiselers who made certain that they bilked only those people who were bigger crooks than themselves! The sophisticated swindlers in question were Marcel St. Clair (Charles Boyer), Alex Fleming (David Niven), and Tony Fleming (Gig Young).

On the opposite end of the scale, there were a handful of very weighty shows this season, programs of the "East Side/West Side" school. These series managed to avoid the brooding pessimism of the Scott production by presenting the same hard-hitting realism, but with a strong leading player and flawed costars. Basically, this was the format that had proven so successful in "Combat." Indeed, one of these newcomers was a Quinn

Flipper.

David McCallum, Robert Vaughn, and Leo G. Carroll of "The Man from U.N.C.L.E."

Martin war series entitled "Twelve O'Clock High," adapted from the classic 1949 Gregory Peck film. This time it was Robert Lansing in the fore as Brigadier General Frank Savage of the 8th Air Force B-17 bomber group, stationed just outside of London. Costarred were the late John Larkin as Major General Wiley Crowe, Frank Overton as Major Harvey Stoval, Lew Gallo as Major Joe Cobb, and Barney Phillips as Major "Doc" Kaiser. Enlivened by stock footage of actual aerial battles, "Twelve O'Clock High" was not a series in which the Nazis were our only enemies. More often than not, we were thwarted by our own greed, uncertainty, or cowardice. Indeed, in the very first episode, the grim, steel-eyed Lansing tore into guest star Paul Burke (as Capt. Gallagher), informing him that "today, you have made the worst enemy you will ever have. You are a disgrace to the uniform that I hate to share with you. I hate you more than a Nazi because you're supposed to be on our side." Ironically it was Burke who, in a different role, would inherit the series when Lansing left after the first season. His departure was dictated by the moving of the show from a 10:00 to a 7:30 berth, and network executives were afraid that young audiences would be unable to identify with a Brigadier General. Quite understandably, Lansing was so peeved with this ruling that he refused to do even an occasional guest spot, and had to be written out of the series entirely courtesy of an airplane crash.

However, if "Twelve O'Clock High" and "Combat" shared a common people-oriented spirit, there was an even stronger bond between "East Side/West Side" and the laudable "Slattery's People." Theoretically, "Slattery's People" began where Scott had hoped to see Neil Brock end: as a state legislator. One must wonder,

Gig Young, Charles Boyer, and David Niven as "The Rogues."

however, whether or not Brock could have made the transition. Slattery (Richard Crenna) was a lawyer, and had always been involved with the more statistical side of life. He could afford to be idealistic, since he dealt with appointees, state employees, and lobbyists, rather than with welfare recipients. The rarefied air of this ivory tower was good for his positive, crusading instincts. Brock was a man of the street. Nor was Slattery a loner like Brock; he depended upon his polished staff and fellow legislators for support on the job. And for advice. Guest-starring as a veteran legislator, James Whitmore gave him perhaps the best guidance he would ever receive by saying, "Beware of young legislators riding white horses; it may be a dye job." In any case, Slattery did address himself to the common man as best he knew how, and gave viewers a noble, if implausible, figure of a dedicated politician working for the public.

Other serious and generally responsible programs that season were "Profiles in Courage," a "Great Adventure"-ish omnibus based on John F. Kennedy's Pulitzer Prize winning book, and which told the stories of heroic Americans; and "The Reporter," starring Harry Guardino as Danny Taylor, a young, up-from-the-streets newspaperman who broke stories that no one else would touch. Gary Merrill appeared as his mentor, Lou Sheldon. This was also a season of more frivolous heroes, although, once again, programers did a thorough hatchet-job on the pilots that were particularly empty— such as the story of free-lance frogman Johnny Polo and Jack Lord's Irish sea captain "Yankee Trader"; or heavy-handed—like William Shatner as "Alexander the Great," Stirling Silliphant's "Sinbad," or James Michener's "Focus on Adventure," about a globe-skirting photographer. Yet, half of the efforts that did make it past the preliminary judging and into the fall lineup found their stays to be brief. For a short time, youngsters or fantasy-seeking adults could enjoy the adventures of "Johnny Quest," a Hanna-Barbera

Robert Lansing of "Twelve O'Clock High."

Fess Parker as Daniel Boone with guest star Ethel Waters as Mamma Cooper.

Craig Stevens as Mr. Broadway.

("Flintstones") cartoon series about a young boy who traveled the world over with his scientist father. For the ladies in the audience, there was Craig Stevens as Mike Bell, "Mr. Broadway." Bell was a slick New York City press agent who spent his days protecting show-business personalities from sneaky industry types, and his nights romancing women and avoiding the vengeance of those whom he had thwarted during the day. He eluded them all with ease, but could not escape Mr. Nielsen. Meanwhile, the other two action-hero debuts, "Daniel Boone" and "Voyage to the Bottom of the Sea," enjoyed long and fruitful runs.

"Daniel Boone," with Fess Parker in the lead, repeated the success of Disney's "Davy Crockett." Not only did it have Parker, but the actor made certain he retained those Crockett elements that had made the Disney series a success. Despite the fifty-year span that separated Boone from Crockett, Parker wore the same clothes—from the famous coonskin cap to the sweat-and-mud-stained buckskins—spoke in the same drawling jargon shot through with conviction and vision, and carried himself just as tall as Crockett. All of which might lead one to ask why he didn't simply do an out-and-out Crockett series. The answer, of course, was that while the name belonged to history, the Parker characterization was owned by Disney. As Parker tells it:

In 1963, NBC reran *Crockett* in color, and it wound up in the ratings' top ten. Naturally, I wanted to do either a feature film or a TV series on Crockett. I consulted with my friend Mr. Disney, but Mr. Disney said he was not interested. My lawyers told me that Disney might sue if I proceeded with my own Crockett series, so producer Aaron Rosenberg and I sat down to decide who and what else was like Crockett. We fastened on *Daniel Boone*.

Helping Parker protect the fortified settlement of Boonesborough, Kentucky, were Albert Salmi as his sidekick Yadkin, Ed Ames as the Oxford-educated halfbreed Mingo, Patricia Blair as his wife Rebecca, Veronica Cartwright as his daughter Jemima, and Darby Hinton as his son Israel.

Abandoning the past for the future, we find that Irwin Allen, the commercial wizard behind such motion pictures as *The Poseidon Adventure* (1973) and *The Towering Inferno* (1974), had turned his 1961 film *Voyage to the Bottom of the Sea* into a popular weekly series. In the movie, the atom-powered submarine *Seaview* journeyed to the North Pole to fire a missile at the Van Allen radiation belt and save the earth from incineration. Initially, the series was considerably less exotic, with the men of the *Seaview* mainly involved in stopping enemy saboteurs and spies. By the fifth season, however, Admiral Harriman Nelson (Richard Basehart), Commander Lee Crane (David Hedison), and Lt. Commander Chip Morton (Bob Dowdell) were leading their submariners against men from the future, beings from other worlds, and even marionette duplicates of the crewmembers, strange creatures bent on killing their human lookalikes. Yet, no matter how far-fetched the program became, it was always entertaining and produced with immaculate care.

An interesting regression took place in 1965. Superficially, it involved the fact that seven of the fifteen new hero series were Westerns. More importantly, almost half the new shows were also about dour, very introspective, characters. It was as though they were reflecting a national consciousness, looking into mankind's past, present, and soul, and trying to find the reasons for our many failings. In a spiritual sense, our heroes reflected the rebuilding process that took place in the wake of the Kennedy assassination.

One cannot more succinctly delineate this character in search of meaning than Rod Serling did with his half-hour series "The Loner." Lloyd Bridges starred as William Colton, a Civil War hero who was sick of war. Resigning his commission at the cessation of hostilities, he headed West "to get the cannon smoke out of my eyes,

the noise out of my ears, and maybe some of the pictures out of my head." Naturally, he was not destined to taste this inner peace. Traveling from town to town, he found only pain or the tough scar tissue that had grown around old wounds. However, while this was depressing for Colton, it was an actor's paradise. There was meat enough to create a substantial television tragedy, although the possibilities alone had not been enough to lure Bridges back into a series. "It bugged me quite a bit," he said,

that the guy didn't have any definite background, other than the Union cavalry—even more that he wasn't definitely headed anywhere. But Rod kept telling me to let him worry about the character, just to trust him. And you know something? I did.

Bridges had come to "The Loner" in a blur of activity that saw Serling's four-year-old, hour-long concept cut to an half-hour, sold as a series without a pilot film—CBS wanted a Western to fill a sudden vacancy in its schedule—and Bridges, a millionaire from "Sea Hunt," involved in other projects. But there was the undeniable allure of the excellence that followed Serling wherever he went—from "The Twilight Zone" to the dozens of topnotch scripts such as "Requiem for a Heavyweight," which he had done during the early days of television. Bridges admits, "Rod was the main reason I did the series. With him writing seventy-five percent of the scripts, I knew I'd be in a quality show." Unfortunately, viewers were not interested in Serling's joyless saga, Bridges was angry at the gunfights network executives forced on the series, and the project evaporated after its first season, replaced by a game show.

Like "The Loner," "Branded" and "A Man Called Shenandoah" were also Westerns based on the "search" theme. Unlike "The Loner," however, they had an undercurrent of dignity and romance, respectively, which always left the viewer feeling optimistic. "Branded" was Keven Joseph Aloysuis "Chuck" Connors' third TV series, the sad tale of soldier Jason McCord, the lone survivor of the Indian massacre at Bitter Creek. Returning to the fort, McCord was wrongly accused of deserting his men and was dishonorably discharged, or "branded," as the case may be. Armed with the cavalry sword broken by his superior, McCord spent the next few seasons roaming the West in search of a home and defending his honor. Not bad, except that it was unfortunate how many people he had the bad fortune to meet who had lost a friend or relative at Bitter Creek! A similar suspension of disbelief was required by "A Man Called Shenandoah." Robert Horton starred as the

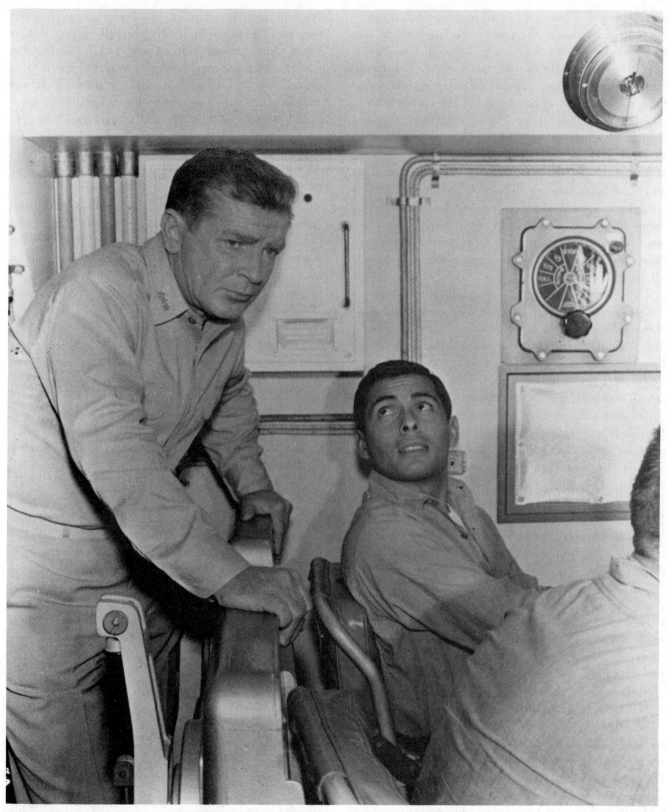

*Richard Basehart (standing) in an episode of "Voyage to the
Bottom of the Sea."*

nameless hero, a man shot in the head and left to die on the prairie. Discovered by a pair of Buffalo hunters, who had hoped there would be a price on his head, the cowpoke was brought to town and revived. The sheriff found nothing on him, although the wounded man would have preferred otherwise: he could remember nothing about his past. This aspect of the show really pleased star Horton: "I got out of *Wagon Train* because the conflicts were all on the outside. In *A Man Called Shenandoah*, however, the hero has inner needs. And they reach out and make the audience pull for him." Naturally, in every episode, "Shenandoah" was always finding someone who "knew him when . . .," but they inevitably died with his name and identity unspoken. When the show expired, Shenandoah was still a man without a single clue about his past.

The remaining seekers of 1965 had a somewhat more awesome playground then the old West, as the Robinson clan of planet Earth found themselves "Lost in Space." This Irwin Allen series, based on the comic book "Space Family Robinson," starred the stalwart Guy Williams as Professor John Robinson and Mark Goddard as Major Don West, leaders of an expedition that was intended to colonize an alien world. Unfortunately, an enemy agent, Dr. Zachary Smith (Jonathan Harris), sabotaged the craft, dooming it to wander aimlessly among the stars. A lone justice was that the prissy Smith was trapped onboard. Also along for the ride were the remaining Robinsons—Mrs. Maureen Robinson (June Lockhart), Judy (Marta Kristen), Penny (Angela Cartwright), and Will (Billy Mumy), as well as a robot whose computer mind was filled with such ready jibes as "You can lead a robot to water but you can't make him compute" and "Ours is not to question why, ours is but to do or be deactivated." The format called for the Robinsons to stumble upon a new planet every other week, which made for colorful if far-fetched adventure. As with "Voyage to the Bottom of the Sea," the production values were striking, and the heroics were portrayed on a grand, one-dimensional scale.

When it comes to men on the run, one would think that "The Fugitive," "Shenandoah," et al, had touched all the bases. Not so. That season there was also Paul Bryan (Ben Gazarra), whose lot was to "Run for Your Life." Only this time it was not a relentless police lieutenant dogging our hero's footsteps, but death itself. When it was determined that Bryan was terminally ill and had only two years to live, he decided to abandon his home and job and spend whatever time he had left traveling the world in search of adventure, wine, and women. He found these adjuncts in abundance, but for Gazarra they

were nothing more than window dressing. Singling out those same qualities in Bryan that had excited Robert Horton about "Shenandoah," Gazarra said, "I refused to be a shadowy leading man who asks the guest stars questions so that they could act up a storm. That was *Arrest and Trial*." This time, the distinguished actor wanted a vehicle that offered "situations where the human condition could be exploited and explored." "Run for Your Life" was certainly a classic showcase for this, although one need not be a vagabond to probe the human persona.

There were other series with introspective and exciting characters, such as William Shatner as Assistant D.A. David Kester in the short-lived "For the People," and Christopher Jones as the colorful Robin Hood of the West in "The Legend of Jesse James." However, these shows lacked the sweep of "Run for Your Life." And this scope was the primary reason that Bryan was able to survive for five seasons, proving that Nielsen can be more powerful than medical science. There was always a change of scenery to keep the show from stagnating. This is a quality that has historically worked for TV series, although few programers have come to understand this. For example, everfresh and exotic locales was one of the elements that made "I Spy," another of this season's entries, a runaway hit. The other popular components in the well-oiled "I Spy" machine were its stars. This "spyance fiction" series, as *TV Guide* christened it, was the first dramatic show to feature a black performer, Bill Cosby, in a leading role. Remember that this was less than two years after a goodly number of network affiliates refused to broadcast "East Side/West Side" because of its mature approach to the changing image of the black American. Cosby portrayed Alexander Scott, a Rhodes Scholar and partner in secret agenting with Robert Culp, as Kelly Robinson. Their disguise was that of a tennis bum (Culp) and his trainer-masseur, their court was the world, and the combination of lush scenery and rapid-fire quips exchanged by Culp and comedian Cosby made even the standard foreign intrigue plots seem fresh and original. Besides, how could one not tune in to a series that featured an installment like, "Carry Me Back to Old Tsing Tao?"

Somewhere to the left of the irreverent and enlightened Culp-Cosby classic was the considerably less orthodox, almost Bohemian, "Trials of O'Brien." This was the series that gave actor Peter Falk the unkempt, absent-minded image that carried through to his later "Columbo" triumph. Indeed, the one real difference between the two series is that "Trials of O'Brien"

Efrem Zimbalist, Jr. in "The FBI." This multipart episode, costarring Telly Savalas, Walter Pidgeon, Celeste Holm, and Susan Strasberg, was edited into a feature-film entitled "Cosa Nostra: An Arch Enemy of the FBI."

premiered some seven or eight years ahead of its time. Falk portrayed crap-shooting, fast-talking trial lawyer Daniel J. O'Brien. who was beset by gangsters on one side, legal opponents on another, clients on a third, and his ex-wife Katie (Joanna Barnes) on still another. Yet, he somehow managed to keep them all at bay with excuses like the following, which he once gave to Katie: "If I pay you the alimony, then I can't pay the bookies. And if I can't pay the bookies, they'll have me killed." How does one argue with logic such as that? The series was shot entirely in New York City, in whose pool halls the tough, Cagney-esque Falk seemed perfectly at ease; certainly more so than he was in the city's stately courtrooms. Despite O'Brien's very puggish attitude, however, series director Franklin J. Schaffner (*Patton, Planet of the Apes*) observed that "Peter may appear to be doing everything off-the-cuff, but there is a strong intuitive intelligence operating there." Falk himself felt that

the character is a serious one, but he can be played for laughs. About three laughs for every moment of seriousness. No crusading: nothing but a straightforward offering of entertainment, because when they start to get serious on TV, they either get pretentious or they take a simple subject and over-complicate it with a lot of jazz it doesn't need. Each *Trials of O'Brien* show has a point, but we keep it comic as well as meaningful.

Meanwhile, there was still a great and ongoing affinity for more traditional heroes, which is why "The FBI" became one of the most popular "police" shows in television history. Producers had long been wooing Bureau director J. Edgar Hoover to cooperate and open his files for TV dramatization, but he refused. He was worried that the tube would wreck the integrity of his institution. Only when Quinn Martin and the tightly knit Efrem Zimbalist, Jr. associated themselves with an FBI teleproject, did he agree to work with the medium. Even then he ran a thorough check on the backgrounds of everyone concerned, just to make certain that there was no one in the cast or crew who might embarrass the Bureau.[23] The focus of the series was Inspector Lew Erskine (Zimbalist), a thirty-year man whose wife had been killed in a 1944 ambush. This low deed toughened Erskine to the point where Zimbalist inherited a character who was less a man than an automaton. Although this made the actor's contribution little more than chemical, it did provide for an excellent foil with his usually wild-eyed adversaries. Dressing the program were props, plots, and dialogue that were absolutely authentic; Zimbalist went so far as to spend a week at the Bureau Academy in Quantico, Virginia, to whet his humorless Erskine on the FBI's concrete breeding grounds. Despite this very businesslike atmosphere, the program was realistic and offered staccato-paced scripting and absolute professionalism in its production—all of which helped to keep it alive for a remarkable seven seasons.

The rest of that season's heroes were either moderately serious or moderately absurd. On the more conventional side were "The Big Valley," "Laredo," and "Convoy." The scamps were "Honey West" and—no relation—"The Wild, Wild West." All that can be said on behalf of "The Big Valley" is that Barbara Stanwyck was on hand to lend the series class. She starred as Victoria Barkley, the iron-willed matriarch of the Barkley Ranch in San Joaquin, California, circa 1870. Costarring in this bland attempt to build another "Bonanza" were Richard Long as the cool-headed son Jarrod, Peter Breck as the hot-headed son Nick, Lee Majors as the illegitimate and rambunctious half-brother Heath, Charles Briles as the sensitive son Eugene, and Linda Evans as the impulsive daughter Audra. "Laredo" was a more entertaining effort about the brawling, free-wheeling Texas Rangers Reese Bennett (Neville Brand), Chad Cooper (Peter Brown), Joe Riley (William Smith), and their commanding officer, Parmalee (Phillip Carey). Unfortunately, while these characters were more human than those of the vintage "Tales of the Texas Rangers" series, the scripts were simply elaborations of standard Western themes. In this respect, at least "Convoy" had the advantage of being built around a fresh subject, as Commander Dan Talbot (John Gavin) led his fleet of freighters through the stormy waters of World War II. John Larch and Linden Chiles costarred as Capt. Ben Foster and Chief Officer Steve Kirkland. However, the producers still fumbled the ball, as "Convoy," with all of its potential, developed into nothing more than a second-rate "Wagon Train." The Indians were now U-Boats; their arrows, torpedoes; and the scouts, destroyers; but the format was unmistakable.

"Honey West" was at least an energetic program, with the first featured heroine, per se, since Annie Oakley. Ms. West was originally seen in a supporting role on "Burke's Law," where the lady agent proved so popular that she was given her own show. Anne Francis, a 5'7" actress whose principal fame to date had been as the star of the science-fiction classic *Forbidden Planet* (1956), was Honey West, the kung-fu expert who inherited a detective agency from her father and decided to keep the place open. John Ericson was costarred as her associate, Sam Bolt, and the series was played with the same farcical slant as its parent program. However, Honey West's greatest concession to the mode of the day was the star's secret agentish alligator handbag, complete with a pearl-handled derringer, a .38 caliber pistol, pick locks, tranquilizer bullets, a bug in the shape of an olive-on-a-toothpick for spying on intimate restaurant rendezvous, a lipstick radio transmitter, and a sunglasses sending and receiving unit. It was all very slick but, like its thematic antecedents, was also very shallow. The same can be said of "The Wild, Wild West," a Western with Robert Conrad as James T. West, an undercover agent who traveled the frontier of the 1870s onboard a private railroad car. His sidekick was that master of disguise Artemus Gordon, played by Peter Gunn's erstwhile aide, the excellent Ross Martin. Armed to the teeth with

Ross Martin (left) and Robert Conrad of "The Wild, Wild West."

smoke bombs under his holster, a two-part derringer in his bootheels, a sword in his pool cue, and a skeleton key behind his lapel, West took on any and all adversaries of these United States. And hokey though the series was, with gimmicks and anachronisms galore, the "Man from U.N.C.L.E." crowd loved it. Good thing, too. Had the ratings taken a dip, star Conrad may have begun recruiting viewers with his sword cue. Or was it a mis-cue? With all due respect, it is the author's duty to note that Conrad's attitude toward the show's personnel left much to be desired. "I like being a star," he told *TV Guide,*

> I like the people I work with, and they like me. If somebody doesn't like me, I don't want him making a living off something I'm connected with. You talk to anyone on this set who doesn't, and let me know. I'll get rid of him. I can't be bothered trying to win them over. I haven't time for that.

Funny: we always thought that the ability to reason with fellow creatures was one of the things that distinguished humankind from the other animals.

Before leaving 1965, two series that didn't make it into a network lineup deserve our attention. The hour-long pilot for Joseph E. Levine's "Hercules," with Gordon Scott, was one of the most spectacular undertakings in television history and remains a literate interpretation of an oft-maligned subject. It would have been interesting to see how these confused transitionary years would have reacted to a serious and well-made epic about a mythological hero. Another excellent test film was for a then unique type of hero known as "The Ghostbreaker." Kerwin Mathews, star of such fine films as *The Three Worlds of Gulliver* (1959) and *Seventh Voyage of Sinbad* (1958), portrayed a distinguished parapsychologist who went around investigating haunted houses. As an occult mystery, "The Ghostbreaker" was superb and, unfortunately, predated the supernatural craze by several years. However, anyone who was able to remain calm in the face of a rift between our world and the next—the way Mathews did—is deserving of mention in a volume on the hero, television or otherwise.

By anyone's standard of measure, 1966 was *the* year for the television hero. More specifically, it was The Year that Batman Built. The resilient comic-book character came to television in the company of such distinguished series as "Tarzan," "Star Trek," "Mission: Impossible," "The Avengers," "The Saint," "The Green Hornet," and eighteen other newcomers. Actually, "Batman" premiered earlier than the rest, a part of the first concerted "Second Season" push, meant to fill the spots in January that were left vacant by disasters from the previous Fall.

Anne Francis as the deadly Honey West.

When first assigned the task of bringing "Batman" to television, producer William Dozier was

taken aback. *Batman* was simply not in my ken. But ABC had bought the concept without any idea of what to do with it. So I bought a dozen comic books and felt like a fool doing it. I read them—if that is the word—and asked myself what do I do with *this*? Then I hit on the idea of camping it.

And "camp" it they did, staging "Batman" like a hopelessly outdated movie serial and playing it *so* straight that it was hilarious. Dozier even retained the cliffhanger format of the serials, presenting "Batman" in a pair of semiweekly, half-hour segments. The first chapter would leave Batman (Adam West) and his aide Robin (Burt Ward) facing certain death in some dastardly trap, from which they would always escape at the beginning of the second installment. These traps, of course, were concocted by each week's guest villain. And once the series had become an overnight sensation, playing an evildoer on "Batman" was a status symbol in Hollywood. Among the featured nasties were Frank Gorshin as the Riddler, Cesar Romero as the Joker, Burgess Meredith as the Penguin, Julie Newmar as the Catwoman, Otto Preminger as Mr. Freeze, David Wayne as the Mad Hatter, Liberace as Chandell, and many others.

Lewis Wilson as one of the two serial interpretors of "Batman."

When they were not parading around in costume, Batman and Robin were millionaire playboy Bruce Wayne and his young charge, Dick Grayson. Living with them at stately Wayne Manor, on the outskirts of Gotham City, were their butler, Alfred (Alan Napier)—the only living soul privvy to the superheroes' alter egos—and Aunt Harriet (Madge Blake). "Batman's" liaison at police headquarters were Commissioner Gordon (Neil Hamilton) and Chief O'Hara (Stafford Repp). By its third of four seasons, "Batman" had been cut back to one self-contained half-hour per week, with extra color provided by the addition of Batgirl (Yvonne Craig) to the cast. In "real" life, the cowled heroine was Barbara Gordon, the aloof and proper librarian daughter of Commissioner Gordon.

The success of "Batman" sent programers running for their Xerox machines. Dozier, of course, was one step ahead of them all and had "The Green Hornet" ready for broadcast by September. Unlike "Batman," however, Dozier wisely avoided a camp approach to his adaptation of the radio and comic-book hero. According to star Van Williams, "The Green Hornet" had to be done straight because the character just didn't have that pompous flair of the more dynamic "Batman." "In fact," Williams

Adam West as Batman.

Burt Ward as Robin.

observed, "the *Green Hornet* is a pretty dead-pan guy." A veteran of two movie serials, rather droll affairs entitled *The Green Hornet* (1940) and *The Green Hornet Strikes Again* (1940), the character was created by the same crew that gave birth to "The Lone Ranger." In fact, he's Ranger Reid's great grandson! Although this relationship was never explored in the TV series, Britt Reid, publisher of the great metropolitan newspaper *The Daily Sentinel*, was very much like his noted ancestor. Both men disguised themselves by masking their faces and fought evil with a "trademark" weapon: silver bullets for the Ranger and Britt's hornet's sting, which used

high-pitched sound to break down doors or render people unconscious. Like the Lone Ranger, the Green Hornet rode a "horse," although in name only: the sleek Black Beauty was an automotive armory, complete with guns, a smoke screen, infrared lights for night vision, an airborne camera to keep track of fleeing adversaries, and so forth. Finally, each lawman operated with the assistance of a minority sidekick. Assisting the Green Hornet in every adventure was his own "Tonto," an Oriental chauffeur and expert at kung fu named Kato. Kato was played by the late cult hero Bruce Lee, who made the series' fight scenes among the most sensational

The famous Batmobile.

of such footage ever shot for television. In fact, when Lee became one of the top theatrical attractions of the early seventies, several "Green Hornet" episodes were edited into a feature-length film and released under the title of *Kato*. Costarring in the series were Wende Wagner as Casey Case, Reid's personal secretary at the newspaper; Walter Brooke as D. A. Scanlon, the only man who knew that the Green Hornet and Britt Reid were one and the same; and Lloyd Gough as *Daily Sentinel* reporter Mike Axford, who was convinced that the emerald avenger worked for the underworld.

Although none of this season's other heroes were as farout as the Dozier twins, there was still a fair share of very exciting business on display. "T.H.E. Cat," for example, was the name of a cat burglar turned crime-fighter. Thomas Hewitt Edward Cat (Robert Loggia) remained on call at an alley-bordered dive called the Casa Del Gato, where he was at the disposal of Capt.

McAllister (R. G. Armstrong) of the metropolitan police. When summoned to action, Cat garbed himself from head to toe in black and, grapnel in hand, sallied forth to exploit his peculiar talents. The show was not a ratings success, although two years later an identical concept made a hit of "It Takes a Thief." The difference between the two was "T.H.E. Cat's" low-keyed, very mellow environment. The show featured nothing that was even remotely rhapsodic, the action was vicious, and the criminals were gutter-spawned. There was rarely a female consort for Cat, and our hero was an artist at what he did, rather than a showman like the protagonist in "It Takes a Thief." And much of this unusual atmosphere was provided by the ever-distant Loggia, of whom producer Boris Sagal said, "He has the cat mystique, and moves like greased lightning." The former star of *Elfego Baca* was indeed superb and created a character who, like his namesake, didn't have to bare his claws for the audience to know they were there!

Van Williams as The Green Hornet, holding his Hornet's Sting, and Bruce Lee as Kato.

Ron Ely (right) as Tarzan, with guest stars Woody Strode and Julie Harris.

In vivid contrast to Cat was "Tarzan," who, swinging nearly naked through the trees, bleached golden by the sun, and forever bellowing his ape-inherited cry, was anything but subtle. "Tarzan" came to television more or less as created by pulp novelist E. R. Burroughs. Gone was Johnny Weissmuller's monosyllabic brute: Ron Ely's ape-man was articulate, wily, strong, and graceful. He was also Jane-less, but had many lady friends during the healthy run of the series. "Boy," too, was thankfully missing, although a native orphan named Jai (Manuel Padilla Jr.) joined Tarzan on most of his adventures. The chimpanzee Cheetah survived the transition intact.

"Tarzan" was one of the most expensive series in television history. Shot in Brazil and Mexico, it was beset by such problems as torrential rains, which postponed filming and destroyed an $80,000 village set; electrical generators, which were brought to various locations and failed to function; the stomach disease *turistas*—or was it *tsuris*—which felled entire blocks of the Portuguese-speaking crew; and star Ely himself, who was usually laid up with injuries due to the fact that he insisted on doing his own stunts. "This is the character I became an actor to play," Ely explained. "He is noble, strong, the epitome of a hero. So if it's something I feel I can do, I

Roger Moore as James Bond, a characterization of the same timbre as the Saint.

should do it myself. It's no good selling something that isn't the truth. I want to make the viewer believe that I am *Tarzan!*" Among the more dangerous stunts tried by the future movie Doc Savage were riding a zebra bareback, wrestling a lion, scampering through a climactic fire in a $110,000 village set—after which scene Ely collapsed, his faced blistered by the heat—and swinging from vine to vine. In fact, during one such pass, Ely slipped and fell twenty-eight feet to the ground. The script was rewritten to make a bullet responsible for the accident, and the footage proved quite spectacular to everyone except Ely. "I still have the memory of the ground coming closer," he later said, "and it's a very bad memory to have."

Ordinarily, an hour-long series requires five or six days schooting per episode, but each "Tarzan" program averaged three to four weeks before the cameras. However, it was a hit in the ratings, and inspired a number of pilot imitations: "Tar Gar," starring Mike Henry, the former movie Tarzan who dropped out of the "Tarzan" series two days before it was scheduled to roll—due to litigation over a chimp bite he had received; "Walter of the Jungle"; "Alfred of the Amazon," and "George of the Jungle." Only the last effort, a clever cartoon comedy series from Jay Ward ("Rocky and Bullwinkle") made it to television the following season. The jungle series "Daktari" also premiered in 1966. "Daktari," which is Swahili for doctor starred Marshall

Patrick Macnee and Diana Rigg of "The Avengers."

The stars of "The Time Tunnel," with the titular passageway behind them.

Thompson as Dr. Marsh Tracy, whose job it was to study animal behavior at the Wameru Game Preserve in Africa.

Far removed from the primeval world of Tarzan and his brood was the jungle of the contemporary world. Here, such characters as "The Saint," "The Baron," "The Avengers," and "Hawk" plied their anticrime trade. "The Saint", starring Roger Moore in his third of four television series, was private investigator Simon Templar, while antique dealer and art investigator John Mannering, the Baron, was American actor Steve Forrest. Both shows were filmed and set in England. Also from England was "The Avengers," sophisticated crime-fighters John Steed (Patrick Macnee) and Mrs. Emma Peel (Diana Rigg), a wealthy adventurer and a highly educated, tough-spirited young widow of a famous test pilot. While Macnee would remain with the show through its various incarnations, Honor Blackman, Miss Rigg, Linda Thorson (as Tara King), and, in a 1976 edition, Joanna Lumley would be his lady partners. "Hawk" was a more delitescent mode of hero—Burt Reynolds as the brooding John Hawk, an Iroquois Indian who worked for the D.A.'s office in this filmed-in-Manhattan program.

There was a strange brew in the bulk of this season's heroic series, with the ingredients ranging from Westerns to espionage to cops. And, although the pilots for "Mandrake the Magician" and "Houdini's House" failed to sell, there was magic aplenty in this year's science-fiction entries, "Time Tunnel" and "Star Trek." "Time Tunnel" was Irwin Allen's third concurrent television effort, as Dr. Doug Phillips (Robert Colbert) and Dr. Tony Newman (James Darren) became lost in the fourth dimension after entering the untested, government-sponsored Time Tunnel. Each week the scientists became unwilling heroes as they hopped through time from one calamity to another—from the bombing of Pearl Harbor to the French Revolution to the American Civil War, and so on. The only problem with the show was that Allen insisted on padding each hour-long episode with stock footage from existing films. While this kept the budget down, it also gave the series a disjointed, patchwork quality.

"Star Trek," on the other hand, was a crisp and lavishly mounted epic, detailing the intergalactic adventures of the starship *Enterprise*. Intellectually, the series was light years ahead of most other television fare, although it was the characters that inspired a "Star Trek" cult that today boasts tens of thousands of registered members. Commanding the four-hundred-person-strong *Enterprise* was Capt. James T. Kirk, played by William

From left to right: DeForest Kelley, William Shatner, and Leonard Nimoy of "Star Trek."

Leonard Nimoy as the popular Mr. Spock of "Star Trek."

Shatner. Strong and compassionate, Kirk was a man of the highest moral and heroic fibre. Once, when an enemy hid a phaser—a futuristic hand weapon—somewhere in Kirk's quarters and set it on overload, the captain took the time to get on the intercom and order all personnel to evacuate the area—this, in a situation where seconds might have made the difference between life and death in an hellish explosion. By Kirk's side during the phaser incident, and most every other danger in the series' three-year-run, was the half-breed science officer and second-in-command, Mr. Spock (Leonard Nimoy). Born of a terrestrial mother and a Vulcan father, the alien was every bit as heroic as Kirk, but devoid of human feelings.

Or so he claimed. While his every move and action was dictated by logic, the fact that Spock stuck by Kirk to search for the phaser indicates a throbbing substratum of emotion. Rounding out the showcased crew members were DeForest Kelley as the testy Dr. "Bones" McCoy, Nichelle Nichols as Lt. Uhura of Communications, Majel Barrett as nurse Christine Chapel, George Takei as the Helmsman Sulu, James Doohann as Chief Engineer Montgomery Scott, and Walter Koenig as Ensign Chekov.[24]

Another series that many viewers considered science fiction was "Mission: Impossible," the story of a government agency called the Impossible Missions Force

*Leonard Nimoy as Mr. Spock and Jeffrey Hunter as Capt. Pike
in the first "Star Trek" pilot. Note Spock's more highly elevated
eyebrows, as well as the different uniforms.*

that specialized in—well, in impossible missions. Their projects ranged from convincing a man that World War III had destroyed civilization, to training a cat to perform an intricate burglary. Atypically, "Mission: Impossible" went through an extraordinary number of personnel changes during its seven-year run. The first season saw Steven Hill featured as Dan Briggs, leader of the group. Martin Landau, who had turned down the role of Mr. Spock on "Star Trek," costarred as master-of-disguise Rollin Hand, his wife Barbara Bain was the mannequin-like Cinnamon Carter, Greg Morris was electronics expert Barnard Collier, and weight-lifter

Peter Lupus was Willie, the strong man of the group. By the second season, Hill was gone, his Orthodox Judaism and insistence that he not be required to work after sundown on Fridays or on Saturdays ostensibly holding up production. Peter Graves replaced him as Jim Phelps. By year number four, Landau and Bain had left when budgetary cuts did not allow for the continued purchase of top-notch scripts, and also slashed Landau's appearances by fifty percent. Both he and his wife resigned in protest. Leonard Nimoy, with "Star Trek" grounded, joined the cast as Paris—a master of disguise. He quit after two years, tired of the part. In season number five,

William Shatner in a decidedly un-Kirk-ish pose.

Lesley Warren became a member of the cast playing Dana, until Lynda Day George replaced her in the series' sixth year. Whoever was featured, however, had to play his or her part with grim determination and as second-fiddle to the involved—often convoluted— schemes and gadgets that were employed to fulfill the assignments at hand.

The lingering government-sponsored agents of 1966 were not nearly as popular as "Mission: Impossible." High hopes had been held for "The Girl from U.N.C.L.E.," but the show was a poorly received spinoff of the Vaughn-McCallum series. Stephanie Powers starred as agent April Dancer, and Rex Harrison's son Noel appeared as her aide, Mark Slate. Leo G. Carroll was retained from the original program as Mr. Waverly, as were the U.N.C.L.E. headquarters situated behind a dry-cleaning shop.

Spies operating in World War II did not receive any better reception than the one accorded Miss Powers. Robert Goulet starred as foreign correspondent cum

Allied spy David March in "Blue Light"; American psychological warfare expert Franklin Sheppard (Don Francks), English demolitions man Nicholas Gage (John Leyton), and French arms and armament wizard Jean-Gaston Andre (Marino Mase) worked behind Axis lines under the code name of "Jericho"; and Robert Lansing returned to the series game as "The Man Who Never Was." Filmed under the working title of "The Long Hunt of April Savage," and then "Danger Has Two Faces," this new show—which was unrelated to the WWII novel of the same name by Ewen Montagu—cast Lansing as secret agent Peter Murphy. After the murder of millionaire Mark Wainwright, Murphy assumed his identity, which was an ambivalent disguise from which to spy on the enemy. Dana Wynter costarred as Mrs. Wainwright, who sanctioned the masquerade, and Murray Hamilton appeared as Lansing's boss John Forbes.

Elsewhere, a group of desert fighters known as "The Rat Patrol" had a larger following than their single-season sleuthing compatriots. Engaged in the more

Stephanie Powers transforms her umbrella into a radio receiver in "The Girl from U.N.C.L.E."

explosive task of policing North Africa were the hard-as-nails Sgt. Sam Troy (Christopher George, husband of Lynda Day), Ivy Leaguer Mark Hitchcock (Larry Casey), former moonshine runner Pvt. Tully Pettigrew (Justin Tarr), and the silent but able Englishman Sgt. Jack Moffitt (Gary Raymond)—men who did their best to stop the Afrika Corps detachments of Capt. Hans Deitrich (Hans Gudergast). Unlike "Combat" or "Twelve O'Clock High," however, "The Rat Patrol" was not about men but super soldiers. Not that the overstated abilities of Troy and company seemed to bother star George: "They call the hero bigger than life, but he isn't. There *are* heroes, and they *are* heroic. All you have to do is read the exploits of these men to know how fantastically heroic they were. There's nothing unreal about a hero. That's what a man should be." Which is true, as far as it goes. Unfortunately, George neglected to mention the other half of the hero: the mortal side.

Somewhat naggingly, this same philosophy must also have been the guiding light behind "Garrison's Gorillas," a *Dirty Dozen* takeoff about a lieutenant who led four convicts into battle behind enemy lines. Awaiting the prisoners was parole if they used their individual specialties to serve the Allied cause. Ron Harper portrayed Lt. Craig Garrison, Cesare Danova was the sophisticated Actor, Christopher Carey was the thieving Goniff, Brendan Boone was the athletic Indian named Chief, and Rudy Solari was the streetwise Casino. Meanwhile, putting men like "Garrison's Gorillas" behind bars were Capt. David Young (Bradford Dillman) and Major Frank Whittaker (Peter Graves), in a one-season, filmed-in-England effort called "Court Martial." The season's sole "soldiers of the street" effort was "Felony Squad," headed by detectives Sam Stone (Howard Duff), Dan Briggs (Ben Alexander), and Dan's son Jim (Dennis Cole).

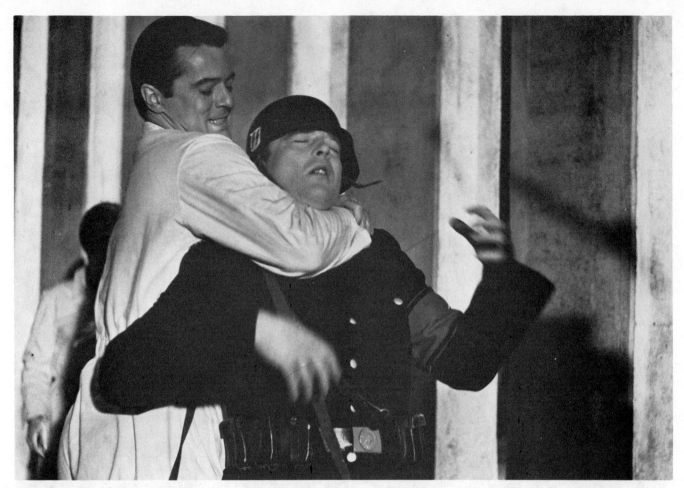

To quote ABC: "Robert Goulet as agent David March, isolated and alone in enemy territory, battles with a Nazi guard in a desperate attempt to accomplish his dangerous mission. This thrilling adventure was filmed in Germany, against the backgrounds where the drama of the Third Reich actually took place."

Christopher George of "The Rat Patrol."

Robert Lansing in "The Man Who Never Was."

113

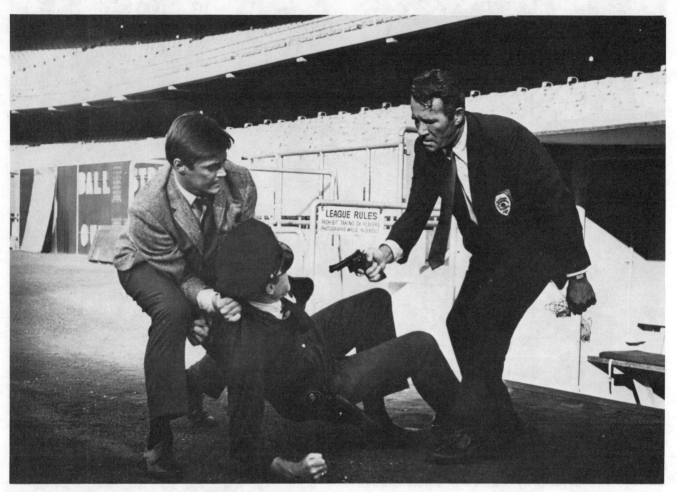

ABC says, "Jim Briggs (Dennis Cole, left) and Sam Stone (Howard Duff) apprehend thief Ben Weil (Kevin Hagen) who has been hiding out in the disguise of a ball park security guard in this scene from the Strikeout *episode of* The Felony Squad.

Out West, there was considerable action in 1966. A total of six new frontier sagas came blazing into view, although none of them survived to the following fall. Best of the lot was the spectacular "Iron Horse," a Charles Marquis Warren series starring Dale Robertson as Ben Culhane, a man who won a railroad in a poker game. What Culhane had to learn about the business made for exciting viewing. Of a semicomedic bent was a contemporary Western called "The Rounders," starring Patrick Wayne—John's son—as Howdy, and Ron Hayes as Ben Jones, precocious ranch hands, and Chill Wills as their boss Jim Ed Love. On the opposite end of the spectrum was David Carradine as the taciturn "Shane," hired hand of the Starett family, in a series based on the classic George Stevens-Alan Ladd film. Speaking for the pioneers, Ben Pride (Barry Sullivan), his sons Tim (Andrew Prine) and Kip (Kelly Corcoran), daughter Midge (Brenda Scott), and friends Chance Reynolds (Glen Corbett) and his sister Elizabeth (Kathy Hayes) faced Kansas of the 1860s in "The Road West". Eighteen-year-old Clayt (Michael Anderson Jr.), sixteen-year-old Kathy (Barbara Hershey), six-year-old Amy (Tammy Locke), and the twelve-year-old twins Little Twin and Big Twin (Kevin and Keith Schultz) were the orphaned "Monroes," youngsters whose parents were killed while crossing the Snake River rapids on their 1870s trek through the Wyoming Territory. Aided by the Indian Jim (Ron Soble), the children decided to puruse their parents' dream of building a home in the West.

Finally, there was the most unusual show of the season, a spoof entitled "The Hero," about the private life of clumsy actor Sam Garret (Richard Mulligan), the man who played the macho and legendary "Jed Clayton, U.S. Marshal" in this series within a series. We mention the show only because Jed Clayton, without the Sam Garret framing story, was the most indestructible Western hero this side of Matt Dillon!

Remarkably, programers went with another six

sagebrush epics in 1967, obviously not content with the Western massacre of 1966. This time, however, they managed to connect with one of the shows! "The High Chapparal" was a hardship-riddled "Bonanza," as John Cannon (Leif Erickson), his tough son Buck (Cameron Mitchell), and his doltish son Blue (Mark Slade) did their damnedest to keep an Arizona ranch from succumbing to draught, Cochise and six hundred restless Indians, and a Mexican cattle baron trying to grab the land. Viewers were relieved to return to their own problems after a visit with the Cannons, and kept the show alive for several seasons. Another Western, "The Guns of Will Sonnett," managed to survive for two full runs, although its ratings were never overwhelming. Walter Brennan had the title role as a lonely old man who scoured the West for his missing son, a gunslinger who went to find fame and fortune years earlier. Before he left, however, the mysterious James Sonnett fathered a son, Jeff (Dack Rambo) who, grown to manhood, accompanied his grandfather on the search. As in "A Man Called Shenandoah," each episode presented Will and Jeff with someone who knew James, agreed to lead them to him, but always died or was killed before making the connection.

Perhaps the most controversial series since "East Side/West Side" was a Western show that arrived and departed this season, a greatly underrated effort called "Custer." The hour-long show was the story of George Armstrong Custer's life after he had been demoted from General to Lt. Colonel and was given command of the hapless Seventh Cavalry. The charge most often leveled against the series was that it glorified a ruthless Indian killer. Glorified him; that is, sanctioned him through deification? No, the series did *not* do that. Portrayed him as he was? Yes. There was never an attempt to defend his atrocities against Native Americans; had "Custer" been filmed with the reverence of "The Great Adventure," then the criticisms would have been justified. But it was the program's intent to balance substantive characterization with bursts of action, which was accomplished without a single concession to dramatic license where history was concerned. The Seventh Cavalry was accurately presented as a collection of the sorriest soldiers the West had ever seen. And Wayne Maunder was superb as Custer, an ambitious, belligerent bastard who carried on a personal war against Chief Crazy Horse (Michael Dante) of the Cheyennes. Never was their conflict sensationalized: each man represented a culture that was butting horns with the other. In this way, "Custer" forced the viewer to examine the biased lessons of history: for the first time in an adult series, Indians

Wayne Maunder subdues an Indian in "Custer." Although critics will claim that this photograph shows the series' low regard for Indians, if one's sympathies lie with the brave, then who is the villain here?

Ralph Taeger as Hondo.

115

were shown to be as clever, and with as much right to life and land as the white man—hardly the orientation one would expect to find in a "glorification" of Lt. Col. Custer. Cofeatured were Slim Pickens as scout California Joe Milner, and Pater Palmer as Sgt. James Bustard.

Unburdened by such considerations, but equally as unsuccessful with critics and viewers alike, were "Hondo," "Dundee and Culhane," and "Cimarron Strip." "Hondo" was based on the 1954 John Wayne film and starred Ralph Taeger as Hondo Lane, an ex-scout for the Confederate cavalry and now a troubleshooter for the United States Army. As if being an ex-Rebel were not trouble enough, Hondo was also a bitter man. His wife, an Apache Princess, had been killed by the army, creating a constant conflict of loyalties as he patroled the Arizona Territory of the early 1870s. Where "Dundee and Culhane" was concerned, however, only the viewer's backside was ever taxed. John Mills, an excellent British actor, seemed terribly bored in his role as, of all things, an urbane British lawyer who traveled about the West with his two-fisted junior partner Culhane (Sean Garrison). Finally, there was the ninety-minute but otherwise unextraordinary "Cimarron Strip," with the talented Stuart Whitman as Marshal Jim Crown of the Oklahoma Territory, circa 1880. Percy Herbert costarred as his boozing deputy, MacGregor.

Putting aside the dust of the prairie, we find that the novelties of 1967 were more unusual than in any previous year, ranging from such subjects as alien beings infiltrating the human race to a chief of detectives operating from a wheelchair. "The Invaders" was a Quinn Martin production in which David Vincent (Roy Thinnes) was the only human being to see the landing of a flying saucer. No one believed him, so Vincent followed up his vision and learned that the aliens were planning to take over the earth. The architect resolved to stop the creatures by himself. Spotting the Invaders wasn't difficult: Caucasian aliens could not bend their pinky fingers, and Black Invaders had all-black palms. However, destroying them was quite another matter; and when the series came to an end two years later, the aliens were still amongst us.

"Ironside" was considerably more down-to-earth, as a sniper deprived San Francisco Chief of Detectives Robert Ironside (Raymond Burr) of the use of his legs. Undaunted, the veteran lawman set up living quarters on the third floor of the police building, from where he continued to fight crime. Aiding his cause were Detective Sgt. Ed Brown (Don Galloway), policewoman Eve Whitfield (Barbara Anderson), and ex-con Mark Sanger (Don Mitchell). Quite remarkably, Raymond

Burr was able to shed the Perry Mason image that had been with him for nine years and gain immediate acceptance in this new role. As Burr explains it:

"In *Ironside*, I've switched from the defense to the prosecution, playing a legendary police detective who becomes a crime consultant following permanant injury by a sniper's bullet. There's more latitude in showing a human being, because he's not tied down to a courtroom. Even so, doing this show is something like doing a Greek Tragedy. You already know what the end will be. And because the action is schematized and predictable, the whole concentration *must* be on qualities of character.

Achieving this orientation, and backed with top-notch, people-oriented scripts, Burr was able to make "Ironside" a steady hit for an incredible eight seasons running.

Of the more exotic miscellania that season, there was both good and bad fare. "Maya" was a particular standout, the enjoyable stories of a courageous American teenager named Terry Bowen (Jay North, TV's Dennis the Menace), who journeyed to India in search of his missing father, a hunter. He was the kind of lad with whom young viewers could identify—and envy. He was free, on his own in an exciting world, and beset by all

Roy Thinnes.

Raymond Burr as Robert T. Ironside.

manner of danger: the stuff of which youthful dreams are made. Accompanying him on these travels were his native sidekick, Raji (Sajid Khan), and Maya the elephant, on whose back they rode through some eye-filling location scenery and well-plotted adventures. Contrarily, "Cowboy in Africa" was a drab, filmed-in-Hollywood affair, Chuck Connors' fourth and most disappointing series. Connors played Jim Sinclair, a champion rodeo rider who was brought to Africa by the British. With the aide of his Navajo buddy, John Henry (Tom Nardini), Sinclair helped Commander Hayes (Ronald Howard) organize a wild animal ranch where food was bred for African villagers. Connors played a

character who was utterly lacking in depth and served as nothing more than a muscular pawn to get the giraffes and lions on screen. Likewise, the huge bear known as "Gentle Ben" dominated the Ivan Tors series that bore his name, about the Florida Everglades and its game warden, played by Dennis Weaver.

Unfortunately, several "Batman"-inspired projects promised to be exciting series, but failed to find a niche in any network schedule. Among them were "Dick Tracy," "The Hardy Boys," "The Shadow," and "Mr. Zero," the last of which was about an alien visitor who came to earth to abolish evil. However, a number of superheroes did make it to the air, although they were not

Don Galloway (left, top), Don Mitchell, Barbara Anderson, and Raymond Burr of "Ironside."

exactly made from the same stuff as the Lone Ranger or Superman. "Mr. Terrific" was a comedy about Washington D.C. gas station owner Stanley Beamish (Steven Strimpell), who donned a scarf and silvery jacket, took a special pill at the request of his government, and received "the strength of one hundred elephants, a nose for scent equal to the sniffers of five-hundred bloodhounds, and the jumping power of a thousand kangaroos," according to a CBS press release. The show was an out-and-out comedy, but a generally puerile one. It's sole redeeming factor was the dry performance by superb character actor John McGiver as Barton J. Reed, head of the Government's Bureau of

Secret Projects. Far superior to "Mr. Terrific" was producer Buck Henry's ("Get Smart") hilarious "Captain Nice," the story of police scientist Carter Nash (William Daniels, in a role originally intended for Tim Conway), who invented a formula that gave him superstrength. As the title song described our hero:

"Look, it's the man who flies around like an eagle! Look, it's the enemy of all that's illegal! Who could it be, this man with arms built like hammers? It's just some nut who walks around in pajamas! That's no nut, boy. That's *Captain Nice*!

Flying through the skies of Big Town, the stalwart Captain faced nemeses that were far more deadly than the routine spies and secret agents tackled by Mr. Terrific. There were mad scientists, assassins, and even a worm who became superpowered after imbibing some of Carter's secret formula. Fortunately, the earthquake-causing annelid was lured to its doom when Carter created a machine that electronically re-created the sound of lettuce crunching. Costarring in this unrecognized classic were Alice Ghostly as Mrs. Nash and Anne Prentiss as Carter's policewoman admirer, Candy Kane. Speaking of Anne Prentiss, her sister Paula was also associated with a comedic superhero as she costarred with real-life husband Richard Benjamin in "He and She." In the series, "He" was a cartoonist who created the television sensation "Jetman," who was played for laughs by Jack Cassidy.

With the exception of "Coronet Blue," the rest of this season belonged to the law, as a private eye, an attorney, and two police shows premiered. First, however, the strange history of "Coronet Blue." This series was originally filmed in 1965, but was held due to its "uncanny" resemblance to "A Man Called Shenandoah," and because the TV executives who bought it decided that they didn't like it! Eleven of the thirteen completed episodes were finally aired that season, and enjoyed a widespread cult following. "Coronet Blue" was the only link that Michael Alden (Frank Converse) had with his past, words he mumbled to a policeman before passing out from a vicious attack from a group of assailants. When Alden awoke, he found that he had amnesia. Although there was never a resolution to the problem, the summer-replacement show brought Converse to the public's attention. This recognition factor helped make a hit of the rival network series "NYPD," which also premiered that season. "NYPD" was a police show that returned to the coarse, realistic production style of "Naked City," filmed entirely on the streets of New York, with plots torn from newspaper headlines. Converse starred as Det. Johnny Corso, Robert Hooks was Det. Jeff Ward, and Jack Warden portrayed their boss, Lt. Mike Haines. The other police series of 1967 was less a debut than a return, as Jack Webb once again took up badge and purpose in "Dragnet." Portraying Joe Friday's right-hand man was Harry Morgan as Bill Gannon. A third police entry, the Gene Roddenberry ("Star Trek") pilot "Police Story," starring Steven Inhat and DeForest Kelley, failed to sell.

Rounding out that odd, potpourri season were "Mannix" and "Judd for the Defense." "Mannix" was the brainchild of producer Bruce Geller ("Mission: Impossible"), the story of a private eye who worked for Intertect, a computer-run detective agency headed by Joseph Campanella as Lew Wickersham. However, this super agency angle proved too cumbersome, and by the second season "Mannix" had become a free-lance sleuth. Mike Connors was Joe Mannix, a modern-day Sam Spade who managed to get into more fist- and gunfights per episode than any other character in television history. Working detectives were constantly decrying the show's lack of realism, but viewers could have cared less. They kept "Mannix" on the air for nine seasons. "Judd for the Defense" was a no less volatile sort, although his explosions were primarily verbal. The dynamic Carl Betz played Clinton Judd, a granite-willed Texas attorney described by series creator Paul Monash as being "bigger than life, high powered, high priced, high tension, and high living." The role was certainly a change for Betz, who had come to the show after spending nearly a decade as Donna Reed's television husband. Stephen Young costarred as Judd's assistant, Ben Caldwell.

In these past few years, we have seen what amounts to the rise and fall of camp in the television hero. To be sure, there were a handful of bold, original dramatic series, just as there would be isolated serio-comic heroes in the years to come. But the flavor of this era covering 1963–1967 was one of, first, lauding, then destroying, then mocking the hero. In subsequent seasons, however, he would be reborn and mutate from a lantern-jawed saint, in such series as "Hawaii Five-O" and "Medical Center," to a victim and, finally, in the midseventies, to an antihero and an iconoclast. But the word for the next few years would be relevance, as another pair of numbing assassinations, a war in Southeast Asia, and riots all over the country inspired producers to search for that elusive commodity within themselves known as a *conscience*.

7

From The Village to Watergate

I am not *a number, I am a* free man!
—*Patrick McGoohan as* "The Prisoner"

Decades hence, if the 1968 television season is remembered for having contributed anything constructive to the medium, it will be for the seventeen-episode run of Patrick McGoohan's British-made metaphoric and frightening series "The Prisoner." Returning home one afternoon, a man (McGoohan) was rendered unconscious. When he awoke, he found himself in an idyllic town known as The Village—actually, Portmeirion in Wales—whose leaders demanded that he supply them with "information." "You won't get it," he promised them and, when he was not being grilled, spent the rest of his time trying to escape. Surrounding our hero in the quaint seaside settlement was a cheerful but vegetablelike lot of people who were all referred to as numbers. McGoohan was #6; the official who was constantly pressing him for information was #2. And each time #2 failed to obtain this amorphous information, either through trickery or drugs, he was replaced by a new #2. The mysterious #1 was not seen until the final episode.

The viewer's logical assumption had to be that "The Prisoner" was a continuations of "Secret Agent," and McGoohan didn't deny this. As both the series' star and producer he said,

> I know that there are places where people who have top secret knowledge of the highest order and want out are kept.

Not voluntarily, but in absolute luxury. There are three in this country—let someone deny it! I know about this because I know someone who used to be associated with the service. As for our hero, he has no idea who has abducted him. They could be his own people. They could be his enemies. Perhaps both. And he has no idea where he is, except that the compound is a completely self-contained village. It could be anywhere in the world, and there is no way of knowing.

McGoohan, however, intended that the message of "The Prisoner" extend beyond the taut drama of each individual episode:

> I've always been obsessed with the idea of prisons in a liberal democratic society. I believe in democracy, but the inherent danger is that with an excess of freedom in all directions, we will eventually destroy ourselves. I think, for instance, we're being imprisoned and engulfed by a scientific and materialistic world. We're at the mercy of gadgetry and gimmicks. In fact, I'm making my living out of a piece of gadgetry, which is a television set. And computers have everything worked out for us; we're constantly being numeralized. The other day I went through the number of units that an ordinary citizen over here is subject to. Including license plate numbers and all the rest, it added up to some three hundred and forty separate digits!

In the series' concluding episode, McGoohan learned that #1 was a raving lunatic in an ape's mask, finally managed to escape from The Village, and returned to his apartment. Or had he really escaped? As McGoohan entered his home, the door closed behind him automatically, just as it did at his residence in The Village.

Tony Franciosa, one of the stars "Name of the Game."

Compared to the entertainment value and food for thought provided by "The Prisoner," every series henceforth will seem anemic. This is not to denegrate such provocative shows as "Name of the Game" and "The Outcasts," both upcoming, but it's like comparing firecrackers to a Saturn V rocket: they both make a bang, but there's a slight difference in magnitude.

"The Name of the Game" was a ninety-minute-long weekly series based on the workings of a crusading magazine empire. One week the foppish publisher, Glenn Howard (Gene Barry), was the center of attraction; the next week ex-FBI man Dan Farrell (Robert Stack), senior editor of Howard's *Crime Magazine,* was in the spotlight; the third week *People Magazine* writer Jeff Dillon (Tony Franciosa) was featured. Susan St. James was perennially costarred as the rotating executive secretary Peggy. Actually, the series was first seen in November of 1966 with the airing of "Fame is the Name of the Game," the movie that started the films-made-especially-for-TV trend. This, in turn, led to the practice of airing pilots as ninety-minute motion pictures in order to gauge the public's reaction before committing to a series. And there was obviously something to this practice, since "Name of the Game" enjoyed a healthy tenure on the tube, as did "Hawaii Five-O" that season, and many of the other shows tested in like fashion.

"Hawaii Five-O" was shot on location in our fiftieth state and detailed the workings of a mythological special investigative branch of the Honolulu police force. The Five-O unit—up-to-date in terms of equipment, computers, and communications—was also made up of men as tough and determined as they come. This was particularly so of the division head, Steve McGarrett (Jack Lord). As producer Leonard Freeman observed, "When he flashes his badge, people believe it." Costarring were James MacArthur as Danny Williams, Kam Fong as Chin Ho, and Richard Denning as the governor of Hawaii.

As percentages go, that was an exceptionally fortuitous year where the TV hero was concerned. Five of the remaining eight shows were hits, spearheaded by "The Mod Squad," Jack Webb's "Adam-12," and "It Takes a Thief."

"The Mod Squad" was one of the early series to combine elements of the rebel hero with an awareness of what young people were thinking in the midsixties. The squad itself was a trio of "under thirties" who had been arrested for minor infractions and were offered an option: either they went to jail or they went to work as undercover cops. They agreed to join the force, but only if they were never required to betray the confidence of friends, or carry guns. Capt. Adam Greer (Tige Andrews) honored this request, since the kids could go places where ordinary plainclothesmen would be conspicuous, and the LAPD had three new members. They were the rootless daughter of a prostitute, Julie Barnes (Peggy Lipton); the wealthy Pete Cochran (Michael Cole), apprehended while stealing a car for a joy ride; and Linc Hayes (Clarence Williams III), who was arrested for participating in the Watts riots.

Somewhat more traditional were the patrolmen of "Adam-12," rookie LAPD officer Jim Reed (Kent McCord) and the righteous but slightly world-weary officer Pete Malloy (Martin Milner). Then there was cat burglar Alexander Mundy (Robert Wagner) who, in "It Takes a Thief," was offered a jail sentence or employment as a daredevil agent—not for the Mod Squad, but for the SIA. Naturally, he took the cloak-and-dagger post, since it not only saved him from prison and sanctioned his trade but brought him wealth and women as well. Shot under the title of "The Magnificent Thief," "It Takes a Thief" was one of this period's few series to embody a flip "Man from U.N.C.L.E." brand panache, and only then in moderation.

Moving from the season's smash hits to more moderate successes, we find Irwin Allen's "Land of the Giants"

Jack Lord of "Hawaii Five-O."

Jack Lord battles with costar Jay J. Armes in "Hawaii Five-O."
The hooks belong to Armes who, despite his handicap, is one of
the world's foremost detectives.

Andrew Duggan as Murdoch Lancer.

and "Lancer." Large on special effects but short on sense, "Land of the Giants" followed the exploits of seven people who, in 1983, passed through a strange spatial disturbance during a suborbital flight from Los Angeles to London. Emerging from their transport, *The Spindrift*, after a crash-landing, the passengers found themselves in a world where everything was of Brobdingnagian proportions. Unfortunately, the formula for each episode boiled down to capture by the giants, followed by rescue and escape, and flat performances by Gary Conway as Capt. Steve Burton, Don Marshall as his copilot, Dan Erickson, and Heather Young as stewardess Betty Hamilton did little to help the situation. Also along for the ride were Deanna Lund as the attractive scatterbrain Valerie; Don Matheson as Mark, the youthful business tycoon; Stefen Arngrim as the young boy Barry; and Kurt Kasznar as the swindler Fitzhugh. Another of Allen's proposed series, "The Man from the Twenty-Fifth Century," failed to find a market. "Lancer" was more credible stuff, set in the lawless San Joaquin Valley of the 1870s. This, of course, was the locale of "The Big Valley," although it was the only thing the programs had in common. The concept of "Lancer" was an interesting one: Murdoch Lancer (Andrew Duggan) had not seen his sons since they were boys. Plagued by land pirates, the rancher located his grown offspring

through Pinkerton Agents and offered to give them each one-third of his sprawling spread if they would help him to manage it. The young men agreed, although they turned out to be fellows of a decidedly different sort: Scott (Wayne Maunder) was a Boston dandy, and Johnny (James Stacy) was a dyed-in-the-wool Westerner, tough and cynical. The characterizations played extremely well against one another, and made "Lancer" one of the finest Westerns to come along in many a high noon.

On the low end of the 1968 Nielsen totem were two bad shows and one good one. The prime cut was "The Outcasts," another courageous attempt by television to bring unwanted realism into American homes. The title characters were Earl Corey (Don Murray), a former Virginia aristocrat, and Jemal David (Otis Young), a former slave. The men found themselves poverty stricken in the post-Civil War West, and formed an uneasy alliance in order to survive. There was none of the false *I-may-needle-this-guy-but-I'd-really-lay-down-my-life-for-him* comraderie, as the men genuinely hated one another. And they seized every opportunity to prove it. "Where'd you learn to shoot like that, boy?" Earl asked his partner after he saved their skins. "Different times, different places," Jemal explained, adding, "but mostly reminding people that I was *not* their boy." On another occasion, as Jemal prepared to ambush a killer in the dark, Earl commented, "Well, you do have a natural advantage, don't you boy? Unless, of course, you smile." Unfortunately, viewers did not regard this kind of exchange as entertainment, nor did they want to know that there really were black cowboys and that they were treated with even less respect than the beleaguered Indian. As a result, the anger-filled but promising "Outcasts" was cast out at midseason.

It is not difficult to see why "The Outcasts" was dropped. It had too much sinew for the average viewer. However, understanding just why programers bought "Man in a Suitcase" and "The Outsider" is not as easily done, especially when they had more diverting fare from which to choose, such as Ivan Tors' submarine adventure "The Deep Lab" and Bill Dozier's "Call of the Wild." "Man in a Suitcase" was another commodity in the growingly redundant tradition of "Branded" and "The Fugitive." Secret agent McGill (Richard Bradford) was dubbed a traitor for not having prevented the defection of a scientist to the Soviet Union. Naturally, McGill was wrongly accused and went looking for the one missing agent who could prove his innocence. By the time this half-season show had run its course, the crucial operative had not been located, and McGill's name, we must assume, remained muddied for all time. "The

Outsider" was an even brittler property—a cross between "The Fugitive" and "Rocky King." Investigator David Ross (Darren McGavin), a hard-drinking, hard-talking private eye, was released from jail after serving time for a crime he didn't commit. Although the experience gave Ross a chance to meet convicts and learn how they operate, he was very bitter about his bad fortune and lived in a world shrouded with a depressing negativism. Strangely, this was an attitude that McGavin saw as positive! "David Ross is a valid, relevant man in the contemporary world," the actor asserted. "He reflects a whole process of alienation that is going on around us daily. Today, we have a whole generation of outsiders." Perhaps. But Ross was a selfish man, which set him apart from even such rebel heroes as "The Mod Squad." In his self-pitying state he managed to alienate not only the characters in his television world but viewers as well.

With so many heroes carried over into 1969, the final year of the decade had little to offer the field in terms of bulk. Popularity and topicality were a different matter altogether. There were seven new shows that season that fall within the boundaries of our study, and one that lies on the outskirts. This peripheral entry was "Bracken's World," the behind-the-scenes story of Century Studios. The regular characters included producers, directors, actors, actresses, and executive personnel, not to mention studio head Bracken. An unseen figure for the first season, Bracken was given substance in year number two by Leslie Nielsen. Theoretically, the very fact that movie people inspire a mixture of awe and adoration among the general public qualifies the "Bracken's World" characters as heroes—but the show itself was nothing more than a glorified soap opera.

The big hits of the year were a pair of medical efforts—"Marcus Welby M.D." and "Medical Center." Where "Medical Center" was concerned, it was close to being "Ben Casey" all over again. Chad Everett played Dr. Joe Gannon who, when he wasn't arguing with his mentor, Dr. Paul Lochner (James Daly), was debating with nurses, patients, or other medical figures. And he was never wrong. Not about treating select diseases with certain drugs, performing surgery when everyone else said not to, or convincing patients that they would live when both the odds and the charts said it was impossible. In fact, the only difference between Casey and Gannon was that Gannon was an emotional man with an inclination toward moralizing. Casey was simply a boor and a know-it-all. "Marcus Welby M.D." was no different where preaching and self-righteousness were concerned, but at least there was a different angle. The series was presented from the point of view of Welby

In a dramatic flourish, CBS declared, "Dr. Joe Gannon (Chad Everett), undergoing a psychological crisis which prevents him from functioning as a physician, returns to the scenes of his childhood to seek the causes of his attitudes toward death which are troubling him on "Medical Center." Gannon as a boy is played by Bret Swanson.

(Robert Young), a Gillespie-esque doctor of the old school who still made house calls and believed in the importance of a sympathetic bedside manner in treating disease. Operating from Santa Monica, California, Welby's credo was "We don't treat fingers or skins or skulls or bones or lungs: we treat people." Assisting the general practitioner on his rounds was a hipper Kildare in Dr. Steven Kiley (James Brolin), who traveled to see his patients via motorcycle. But he was still the uncertain novice like Chamberlain's medic—and every bit as "cute" as far as the ladies were concerned. Thus, while medical shows now dealt with abortion, prostitution, homosexuality, drugs, and even patients who were porno stars, the basics were still the same.

When we talk about characters who rode around on motorcycles, Dr. Kiley was only a dilettante. That season

Russian actress Victoria Fedorova made her first dramatic appearance on American television with Chad Everett in "Medical Center." She portrayed a Russian surgeon who fell in love with Gannon.

also gave us a true "bike bum" in "Then Came Bronson," television's answer to the movies' *Easy Rider* (1968). Jim Bronson (Michael Parks) was a newspaperman who decided to hang up his press card and find himself by biking across America. In this filmed-on-location series, Bronson worked wherever he could find employment, and always became involved with confused peers or itinerant middle-aged folk. In general terms, however, the young man was not unlike the pilgrims who crossed the Atlantic to settle in America: Bronson didn't know what he wanted or what he would find, but he did know that the rat race of society was not for him. He was perhaps the closest to being a counterculture hero that we will find in television's brief history. He was different from the roamers of "Route 66" in that his perspective

was one of nearly a decade later; nor was he a nihilist and a dropout, afraid of work or hardship. And, unlike "The Outsider," he may have been a taciturn young man, but he was selfless in the finest manner of both the hero and of these concerned times.

A pair of aeronautic disasters resulted in shows about human and superhuman heroes this season. "The New People" were the humans, a Rod Serling creation about a clutch of crash survivors stranded on a small and isolated island. This experiment in a forty-five-minute prime-time series would have worked better as a single motion picture, the mixed bag of survivors forming a potentially interesting microcosm of civilization. However, there was nothing for the characters to do from week to week other than bicker and spout rhetoric about society and human nature. Conversely, "The Champions" was a British import blissfully unconcerned with social commentary. Our titular heroes were agents of Nemesis, whose plane went down in the mountains of Tibet.

ABC's blurb: "A beaming Dr. Welby (Robert Young, left), poses for a wedding album photo with the bridal couple: Dr. James Kiley, his associate (James Brolin), and Janet Blake Kiley (Pamela Hensley), Public Relations Director of Lang Memorial Hospital, following their wedding at the famed Wayfarer's Chapel in Palos Verdes, California, in An End and a Beginning *on* Marcus Welby M.D.*"*

Discovered by mystic priests straight from the pages of Hilton, the spies were given great physical strength, superior mental powers, and fantastic endurance, and were returned to England to combat evil in its many forms. Featured as the invincible heroes were Stuart Damon, Sharon Macready, and William Grant. Luckily,

these heavy-handed gimmick series were balanced by two more rounded and involving programs, "My Friend Tony" and "The Bold Ones." "My Friend Tony" was a quiet little detective series about Tony (Enzo Cerusico), the young and trouble-prone legman for a laboratory-bound professor of criminology, John Woodruff (James Whitmore). "The Bold Ones" was far more bombastic, a trilogy of alternating series seen on a triweekly basis and with a great deal of time spent on the production end. NBC had hoped that the variety and quality of the overall presentation would hold a steady audience from week to week, but they were wrong. However, the convenience of this series was that a weak segment could be replaced without upsetting the bulk of the package known as "The Bold Ones."

In "The New Doctors" segment, surgeon Ben Craig (E. G. Marshall), Chief of Surgery Ted Stuart (John Saxon), and Chief of Medicine and Medical Research Paul Hunter (David Hartman) dealt with the scientific and emotional problems of patients at the Benjamin Craig Institute; "The Lawyers" were the conservative Brian Darrell (Joseph Campanella), swinger Neil Darrell (James Farentino), and elder statesman Walt Nichols (Burl Ives) of the firm Nichols, Darrell, and Darrell; and Police Chief Sam Danforth (Leslie Nielsen) and black District Attorney William Washburn (Hari Rhodes) were "The Protectors," an "Arrest and Trial" team. This last segment proved the least popular and was gone by the second season, replaced by Hal Holbrook as Hayes Stowe, the public-minded, hard-fighting elected official in "The Senator." Ironically, "The Senator" would become one of the most acclaimed shows in television history, although the praise did not save it from low ratings and abandonment after a single season.

When the ten 1970 starters went to the gate, there were many network executives betting on one show in particular, an entry which had all the earmarks of commercial viability. "The Young Rebels" had colorful action, with the Colonials versus the British in American Revolutionary Philadelphia; metaphor, in that the questions of young people circa 1777 were the same as those being asked by their modern counterparts; and a pair of handsome leads in Rick Ely and Lou Gossett. Ely played Jeremy Larkin, who posed as a Don Diego-ish ne'er-do-well and lazy man but was, in fact, the head of a band of rebel guerillas known as the Yankee Doodle Society; Gossett was Isak Poole, a slave who bought his freedom and set himself up as a blacksmith; and Alex Henteloff was Henry Abington, a portly Franklin-esque character who had a way with explosives. Yet, with all of this going for it, "The Young Rebels" failed. And so did

Michael Parks and guest star Bonnie Bedelia in "Then Came Bronson."

Darren McGavin as the Outsider.

the other youth-oriented entries of 1970, despite similarly stacked decks: "The Young Lawyers," with Lee J. Cobb as David Barrett, director of Boston's Neighborhood Law Office, which could afford to offer low-cost counsel to the poor because it was manned by law students Aaron Silverman (Zalman King) and Pat Walters (Judy Pace); "The Interns," about the backbreaking life of hospital apprentices—the handsome and earnest Gret Pettit (Stephen Brooks), the sensitive black man Cal Barrin (Hal Frederick), the long-haired and happy-go-lucky Pooch Hardin (Christopher Stone), the newlywed Sam Marsh (Mike Farrell), and their director, the gruff Dr. Goldstone (Broderick Crawford), and "Storefront Lawyers"—which became "Men at Law" by midseason—about the Neighborhood Legal Services operation, which was run by David Hanson (Robert Foxworth), Gabe (David Arkin), and Deborah (Sheila Larkin) from a shabby Los Angeles building. The NLS was able to offer the same services as Boston's NLO because its members, degreed lawyers, worked part-

Dennis Weaver as "McCloud."

time as members of a high-class law firm in a nice part of town.

No one will ever know exactly why these series failed, although its's a good bet that adults didn't want to watch a bunch of wet-behind-the-ears children show the grown-ups "how to do it," while the kids at whom the shows were aimed didn't like their forced relevance, preferring the topical and more credible Smothers Brothers, Dick Cavett, or Rowan and Martin's "Laugh-in." However, audiences also abandoned old and future favorites. Vincent Edwards bombed as "Matt Lincoln," a psychia-trist with a walkin clinic whose motto was "someone cares"; "The Most Deadly Game" failed despite the presence of George Maharis as Jonathan Croft, Ralph Bellamy as Mr. Arcane, and the lovely Yvette Mimieux as Vanessa Smith, master criminologists all; and Burt Reynolds' second show "Dan August" was a short-lived look at the dangerous life of a Santa Luisa, California, detective lieutenant of homicide. After the cancellation of this series, Reynolds decided to do a theatrical motion picture called *Deliverance*, the film that made him an international star.[25] The remaining casualties of 1970

128

were "The Silent Force," a government sponsored anticrime group, with Ed Nelson as Ward Fuller, Percy Rodriguez as Jason Hart, and Lynda Day (George) as Amelia Cole, and Christopher George as Ben Richards, "The Immortal" who, through a genetic fluke, was endowed with blood that preserved him from disease and aging. Like "The Fugitive," Richards was on the run because a dying billionaire wanted to gain this remarkable immunity by draining our hero of his life essence.

NBC, meanwhile, had found a flexible format in "The Bold Ones," and decided to try a similar tack by presenting several so-called miniseries under the banner of a parent show called "Four-in-One." This first year, four series were presented for six straight weeks each. Christening the ninety-minute program in 1970 were "McCloud," starring Dennis Weaver as Taos, New Mexico, lawman Sam McCloud, who was reassigned to Manhattan to study—and inevitably become involved in—big city police work; "Night Gallery," a Rod Serling fantasy anthology; "The Psychiatrist," with Roy Thinnes as Dr. James Whitman, an unorthodox young psychiatrist who was constantly at odds with Luther Adler as his elderly conscience Dr. Bernard Atlman; and "San Francisco International," starring Lloyd Bridges as the appropriately named airport manager Jim Concord, and Clu Gulager as security head Bob Hatten.

In 1971, "Four-in-One" became "The NBC Sunday Mystery Movie," offering three series instead of four, and presenting them in staggered fashion rather than as three solid blocs. "Night Gallery" became a weekly series on its own, and only "McCloud" survived of the remaining three shows. Joining the program were "McMillan and Wife" and "Columbo." A fourth entry, "Cutter," the adventures of black Chicago detective Frank Cutter (Peter DeAnda), did not win a berth. However, the two new entries were immediate hits. Peter Falk played Detective Lieutenant Columbo as he had portrayed Daniel J. O'Brien: a man who gave the every appearance of being a hapless clutz, but really had much on the ball. As Falk saw the character: "He looks like a slob, and most of the time he acts like one. But while he appears to be absorbing nothing, he's actually absorbing everything." On the surface, Stewart McMillan (Rock Hudson) of "McMillan and Wife" was a different breed of cat entirely, the urban police commissioner of San Francisco. However, beneath the polished exterior was a man every inch as dedicated and real as Columbo. "The thing about McMillan," said star Hudson,

is his humanness. He's not Superman. He'd rather be a

Susan St. James and Rock Hudson relax between takes on "McMillan and Wife."

Rock Hudson of "McMillan and Wife."

129

When legends meet: Patrick McGoohan (right) as ad executive and spy Nelson Brenner in "Columbo" tries not to answer Lt. Columbo's questions.

Peter Falk as Columbo, with guest star Robert Conrad.

criminal lawyer still, but the Mayor has talked him into the Commissioner's job. His wife is crazy about him, he's crazy in love with her, and they get involved in these crime situations as a unit. It's all very healthy—nobody is bigger than life. Our reactions are normal and funny.

Susan St. James, fresh from "Name of the Game," portrayed the effervescent Sally McMillan, Nancy Walker was their maid, Mildred, and John Schuck was the police commissioner's right-hand man, Sgt. Enright.

In addition to the pair of "NBC Sunday Mystery Movie" features, fourteen other series made their bow in 1971, only a trio of which survived for extended runs: "Cannon," "Owen Marshall: Counselor at Law," and "Alias Smith and Jones." "Cannon" was a truly remarkable character—the first fat hero in television history. And not only was he fat, but his greatest joy was getting ever-heavier by preparing high-class culinary delights in his Los Angeles penthouse apartment. But his weight didn't prevent Frank Cannon (William Conrad) from running, stalking, and fighting with the best of the private investigators. In fact, it worked to the character's advantage as far as being realistic went. "I think the most interesting thing in the world is a human being," said Conrad, who once earned his living by playing Matt Dillon on radio's "Gunsmoke." "What he looks like doesn't matter. So you might say that the concept of the leading man is broadening out, using that term advisedly."

A similar break with tradition was offered by "Owen Marshall," as star Arthur Hill portrayed the medium's first soft-spoken lawyer, a man who reserved his occasional flares of emotion for climactic courtroom deliveries. Lee Majors costarred as his assistant, Jess Brandon, and Jean Darling was Owen's secretary, Frieda.[26] Finally, a pair of lovable crooks were showcased in "Alias Smith and Jones", a program freely adapted from the hit Paul Newman-Robert Redford film *Butch Cassidy and the Sundance Kid* (1969). Peter Duel starred as Hannibal Heyes, alias Joshua Smith, and Paul Newman lookalike Ben Murphy was Jed "Kid" Curry, alias Thaddeus Jones. The daring outlaws assumed pseudonyms under the governor's promise that if they went straight for a year, he would grant them amnesty. Unfortunately, the format was hastily altered to accommodate Roger Davis as Smith when Peter Duel committed suicide in December of 1971. Smith and Jones returned to their old ways as happy-go-lucky bandits of the Western plains.

There were several new series that, in many cases, were better than the hits, but for reasons of competition or sophistication didn't make it. "Longstreet" was one

Peter Falk as Columbo in formal attire.

such effort, an intelligent and well-made program about a blind insurance investigator. James Franciscus portrayed Mike Longstreet, the bombing of whose home left his wife dead and the sleuth blind. But Longstreet was determined to fight back. Learning to see via his German Shepherd Pax—whose name, of course, is Latin for "peace"—the detective returned to his New Orleans practice. He learned to shoot a gun by concentrating on the sound of enemy fire and, in one episode, even mastered the martial arts under the tutelage of Bruce Lee. The series never harbored a shred of condolement or, conversely, overstated the *I shall overcome* sentiment that was generic to the story: "Longstreet" was simply a

man with guts. As Franciscus observed, "I wanted to play *Longstreet* as a guy coping, not self-pitying." Marlyn Mason costarred as his secretary Nikki. "Sarge" was another fine program, the story of Father Samuel Patrick Cavanaugh (George Kennedy), a policeman turned parish priest. Despite the fact that he was a man of the cloth, Sarge couldn't help getting involved with those of his flock who came to him and needed a lawman as much as a clergyman. What really made the series exceptional, however—apart from some clever and perceptive scripting—was an alternately solemn, sensitive, and explosive performance by Kennedy. Sally Shockley was featured as Father Cavanaugh's secretary, Vallerie.

131

Other above-average series that missed their ratings mark were "Cade's County," starring Glenn Ford as the laconic Sheriff Sam Cade, who patrolled a large slice of the modern American Southwest; "Man and the City," with Anthony Quinn as Thomas Jefferson Alcala, the four-term mayor of a large Southwestern metropolis, who divided his time between big city problems and "people" problems, such as the plight of a deaf mute couple who wanted to adopt a baby, or a political adversary who learned that she had a terminal disease; "Bearcats," featuring Rod Taylor as Hawk Brackett and Dennis Cole as Johnny Reach, adventurers in the Southwest of 1914 who drove around in a bright yellow Stutz Bearcat and did battle with an arsenal of firearms, grenades, smoke bombs, and even a gattling gun; "Strange Report," an English-made series featuring the excellent Anthony Quayle as Adam Strange, a cool, deductive criminologist who, with his boistrous and rugged aide, Hamlyn Gynt (Kaz Garas), operated outside the law; and "Primus," an Ivan Tors *Sea Hunt* update, starring Robert Brown as oceanographer and undersea troubleshooter Carter Primus.

Moving to the aesthetic wastelands of that season, they were four in number and rather costly in terms of both

William Conrad with guest star Leslie Charleson on "Cannon."

production and ego-bruising. Perhaps the most dramatic disappointment was "The Persuaders": seldom has a series gone to bat with two major stars at the helm and struck out as certainly as did this show. "The Persuaders" was a series whose ingredients had been chosen for their individual appeal rather than for their successful interplay. Roger Moore and Tony Curtis starred as Lord Brett Sinclair and Brooklyn-born Danny Wilde, respectively, a pair of wealthy thrill-seekers who lived on the French Riviera. However, with the chemistry of an "I Spy," it might just as well have been Ocean Parkway for all the public cared. James Garner's "Nichols" was another major letdown, a series intended to be the former TV superstar's dramatic return to the medium after a successful movie career. Garner portrayed Nichols, an eighteen-year army veteran who retired at the outbreak of World War I to avoid any violent undertakings. However, Nichols also did not want to work for a living, so he took a job as the sheriff of a small Arizona town. There, he tried to avoid doing his duty at all costs. However, the televiewing public didn't cotton to "Maverick" revisited, so a change was made in the series, a move which can best be described as tacky. Around midseason, Nichols was killed in the line of duty, and his tough, serious-minded twin brother (also Garner) came to town to pick up where his predecessor had left off. The show was cancelled within a matter of weeks.

Like Garner, David Janssen also reached into the past for direction, to the long-mouldered "Treasury Men in Action," which resulted in "O'Hara, U. S. Treasury." Janssen portrayed James O'Hara, an agent whose work for the government brought him in contact with Customs, the Internal Revenue Service, and the Secret Service, on an alternating basis. Despite having the authenticity attendant to most Jack Webb productions, O'Hara was without dimension or a distinctive identity. Contrarily, the problem with Robert Conrad's new show, "The D.A.," was that the series was all Conrad and little else! Even Jack Webb wasn't able to bring this fatuous half-hour drama to earth, as Deputy District Attorney Paul Ryan (Conrad) served as both an investigator and prosecutor in a modern metropolis. Fortunately, the dependable Harry Morgan was on hand as Chief Deputy H. M. Stafford, to help keep things credible while his superassociate was at work. Webb had better luck in 1972 with an unobtrusive effort called "Emergency."

No one had held much hope for "Emergency." It was going against "All in the Family" on Saturday nights, something akin to putting a loaded revolver to your head and pulling the trigger. But the fast-paced drama held its own, the story of Los Angeles county paramedics and hospital emergency personnel. Robert Fuller and Bobby Troup were Dr. Kelly Brackett and Dr. Joe Early; Julie London (Mrs. Troup) was nurse Dixie McCall; and Rudolph Mantooth and Kevin Tighe played John Gage and Roy De Soto, the paramedics. It was Gage and De Soto who rushed to disasters and held down the fort until the more experienced doctors arrived. The team averaged three or four emergencies per hour show. On a similar beat was "Police Surgeon," a Canadian-made series starring Sam Groom as Dr. Simon Locke.

Speaking of "Police Surgeon," it was one of a number of shows packaged in other countries for sale to network affiliates and independent stations. In the case of the "web" subsidiaries, there were half-hour vacancies to fill in prime time, usually 7:30 to 8:00 or 10:30 to 11:00—slots left open for local programming by the networks. Available for these periods in 1972 were "Black Beauty," an English-made series based on the classic horse novel and starring young Judi Bowker as Vicky Gordon; "The Protectors," with Robert Vaughn and Nyree Dawn Porter as sophisticated "Avengers"-ish detectives Harry Rule and the Contessa di Contini; and "The Adventurer," starring Gene Barry as film star Steve Mallan, who also served as an undercover agent for the United States. Available for nonnetwork syndication was the hour-long show "UFO," also an English effort and set in the year 1980. Ed Bishop starred as Commander Ed Straker, head of S.H.A.D.O.—Supreme Headquarters Alien Defense Organization—a unit whose primary function was to use its bases undersea, in earth orbit, and on the moon to prevent the takeover of this planet by a race of green-skinned, pink-eyed, liquid-breathing aliens.

As for the network offerings in 1972, in addition to "Emergency" there were seven continuing series, one new addition to the "NBC Sunday Mystery Movie," a Wednesday-night version of same, and a trilogy of heroes presented under the banner of "The Men."

The fourth member of "The NBC Sunday Mystery Movie" was a Jack Webb production starring Richard Boone as Hec Ramsey, the deputy sheriff of a small Western town at the turn of the century. Hec was a crack shot who hung up his guns when he became critical of the false values that they both enforced and represented. At the same time, he became challenged by the budding and more civilized tools of crime-busting, such as chemical analysis, fingerprinting, and even hoof-printing. However, Ramsey turned to these "toys" more to sate his own fascination than to serve the ideals of justice. For, according to Boone, Hec was a vintage cynic:

> He's dead honest, and walks right through all the standards of Victorian America. He's Paladin from *Have Gun Will Travel*, grown older. If Paladin had lived all those years, he also would have run out of patience with idots, and would've gotten to be as grumpy as Hec. He would have said to the dames, "Lady, you're not in distress. You're just stupid."

Rick Lenz costarred as Oliver B. Stamp, the young police chief who pushed the more rugged Hec around in order to flaunt his authority.

The Wednesday pastiche consisted of "Banacek," starring George Peppard as a Boston-based, very elegant insurance-company investigator, who was constantly referring to and boasting about his Polish ancestry; "Madigan," with film great Richard Widmark as a tough New York City detective sergeant who was always bending the rules to keep criminals in line; and "Cool Million," featuring James Farentino as Jefferson Keyes, a private eye who hired himself out for one million dollars per case, in advance. Along similar lines, "The Men" were Robert Conrad as Jake Webster who, in "Assignment: Vienna," owned a bar in Austria that served as a cover for his U.S. Intelligence work; Laurence Luckinbill as Glenn Garth Gergory, a research expert with a photographic memory and who worked for the government's "Delphi Bureau"; and James Wainwright as Lt. Frank Dain of California's Missing Persons Bureau who, in "Jigsaw," tried to find the missing persons and help put their lives back together. Surprisingly, although "The Men" and "The NBC Wednesday Mystery Movie" had action, expensive productions, and generally good acting, the public rejected both efforts in toto.

The biggest hit of the year was "The Waltons," the story of a Depression Era family living in the Blue Ridge Mountains of Appalachia. Despite the presence of such outstanding performers as Michael Learned as the mother, Ralph Waite as the father, and Will Geer as the grandfather, the series made a hero of the teenaged Walton, John-Boy (Richard Thomas). This character illustrates the difference between those actors who claimed that their hero was credible, and one who truly was. As we have seen, most TV heroes are aggressive and either work for the people or are self-righteous loners. John-Boy was a survivor, which is no less noble but much more realistic, and certainly more human. The survivor is a character for whom existence rather than public service is the norm, which makes him identifiable—although comfortably inferior to the average viewer—and admirable, without being larger than life. Which is not to say that the survivor is "better" than the knightly hero or the rebel hero. They are simply different characters motivated by different sets of circumstances. For example, a contemporary of the Walton family was a private eye by the name of "Banyon." Robert Forster played Miles Banyon as a hard-boiled, no-nonsense loner whom we got to know primarily through his interplay with costars Richard Jaekel as Lt. Pete McNeil, and Joan Blondell as Peggy Revere, the woman who supplied the dick with a new secretary each week. The survivor and the hero. Two ends of the same scale. But there's a middle ground as well. It's an area we've touched on only lightly, a shaded zone of the heroic spectrum that belongs to the antihero.

The antihero, like the survivor, cannot be cut from a standard television-hero cookie mold. He is moved less by a right cause than by something that personally satisfies him, like Hec Ramsey. There is very little of the martyr in him, and he does not necessarily work in the public's best interest. The hero, as personified by such TV characters as Matt Dillon and Ben Cartwright, act selflessly and for the kind of rights guaranteed by the Constitution and the Magna Carta. However, the antihero—such film characters as *Bonnie and Clyde* and *The Godfather*—can *also* inspire a positive audience reaction because the story is told from their point of view. Obviously, however, the antihero must be more fully rounded than the hero: the audience has to know him very well before they will trust and accept him. And one such TV character was Kwai Chang Caine, the Buddhist monk of "Kung Fu."

Caine (David Carradine) had two reasons for leaving China to come to America. First, he was looking for his long lost half-brother. This aspect of the series was primarily a means of moving him from locale to locale each week. Second, he was fleeing the law of his native land, where he had killed a murderer who turned out to be the Royal Nephew. Thus, Caine roamed the West carefully guarding the one advantage he had over the gun-toting rowdies that surrounded him: he was an expert in the martial art of kung fu, which, literally translated, means "accomplishment technique." He called upon this deadly skill only when there was no alternative and would always reach this decision by referring to the lessons that had been taught to him by the Shaolin priest Master Kan (Philip Ahn) when he was a child. In these sequences, Caine was referred to as Grasshopper and was played by Radames Pera.

The antiheroic Caine was not the same as a hero like

David Carradine of "Kung Fu."

Richard Kimble of "The Fugitive," despite the series' narrative similarities. Kimble would always stop his flight from Lt. Gerard to help a fellow human being. Caine would only emerge from his cocoon when he himself was threatened, or his tranquility offended—certainly a new angle for a television protagonist. "When they first brought me the script," Carradine admits,

I couldn't believe the policy-makers would dare something as discerning and aesthetic as this. The main character speaks very little. He's silent and he lives by humility, patience, peace and reverence for all life. He's a low-key, almost a side-line observer of the cruelty heaped on the workers. But he survives on inner strengths. He's on a quest for truth and goodness and will kill only with the greatest reluctance.

When were "Mannix" or "The Untouchables," for all their nobility, ever reluctant to kill?

A milder form of Caine's philosophy could be found in one of the season's two new police shows, "The Rookies." The title cops were three newcomers to the force—Willie Gillis (Michael Ontkean), who was fresh out of college, Terry Webster (George Stanford Brown), who was fresh from the ghetto, and Mike Danko (Sam

Michael Douglas (left) and Karl Malden of "The Streets of San Francisco."

Melville), who was newly discharged from the air force and married to a nurse (Kate Jackson), and who was replaced in 1974 by Bruce Fairbairn as Chris. Their superior, Lt. Ryker (Gerald S. O'Laughlin), was a hardened old pro, the antithesis of the concerned young rookies, policemen who seldom used their guns and were always involved with the problems of minorities, young people, street gangs, etc. However, since its bleeding-heart orientation was simply defined in blacks and whites, the series was ultimately skin deep and unrealistic. Conversely, "The Streets of San Francisco" made no attempt to be relevant. A Quinn Martin production, it emphasized mystery and action all the way, with the brilliant Karl Malden as Det. Mike Stone, and Kirk's son Michael Douglas (producer of the hit motion picture *One Flew Over the Cuckoo's Nest*) as Assistant Inspector Steve Keller. The crucial relationship here was between the two men, and not between the police and their public. As Douglas explained it:

Keller is an enviable role. I don't just say, "Here's the phone, Mike," or serve as his driver, as it were. We're true partners in every sense of the word. I'm the young college educated student of criminology who might have gone into law but wanted to deal with peoples' problems on a different level. Karl's character never went beyond high school, but he learned on the streets. We work together as equals, each contributing what he knows. I respect his experience, and he respects my training.

Filmed on location, what the series lacked in social awareness it made up for with slick storytelling and interesting characterizations.

Another polished program was "Search," the alternating exploits of three secret agents working for the World Securities Organization. Unfortunately, it aimed a very juvenile gimmick at an adult audience with the result that no one tuned in. The twist was that Lockwood (Hugh O'Brian), Nick Bianco (Tony Franciosa), and playboy Christopher Robin Grover (Doug McClure), all had radios implanted in their skulls, miniature cameras

135

Hugh O'Brian strikes a dramatic pose in "Search."

Richard Roundtree as Shaft.

hidden on their persons, and were wired to computers at WSO headquarters that could pump up the carrier's adrenalin or detect the body heat of anyone trying to sneak up on him. The stories were relatively sophisticated, and the characters well defined, but the undisciplined science of the basic concept was strictly from hunger.

The opposite was true of "The Sixth Sense," where a potentially adult topic was given a juvenile perspective. Paranormal research is a potentially dangerous undertaking, since it tinkers with powers far beyond the ken of most human beings. But Dr. Michael Rhodes (Gary Collins), who had ESP and was a professor of parapsychology in the series, went helter-skelter into preternatural situations. Nor did he ever probe the people it effected or their emotions—only the occult events themselves. Thus, while the results were interesting, they were not what they could have been.

And, finally, that season's medical entry did not even merit a pat on the back. "Young Dr. Kildare," with Mark Jenkins as Kildare and Gary Merrill as Gillespie, simply hadn't enough personality to escape the long shadow of its distinguished predecessor. However, if "Young Dr. Kildare" had its problems, imagine the obstacles faced by Monte Markham as he became "The New Perry Mason" in 1973.

Despite an intense performance by the star, an energetic pace, and strong support from Sharon Acker as Della Street, Harry Guardino as D. A. Hamilton Burger, Albert Stratton as Perry's private eye Paul Drake, and Dane Clark as Lt. Tragg, the show was bucking an institution. And so, like General Savage in "Twelve O'Clock High," a good property went down in flames. It was not alone. Another rehash this new season was a translation of the "Shaft" film series to television. Richard Roundtree repeated his role as the black, New

York-based detective whose first of three movies had started the so-called "blacksploitation" craze in motion pictures. These films, which featured such he-man stars as Jim Brown, Fred Williamson, and Jim Kelly, gave black youths very crucial, very personal hero images, despite—or because of—the fact that they fed the fires of racism by portraying most white men as evil. Of course, when "Shaft" came to TV, this contemporary mythology was obfuscated, leaving John Shaft, superman, to take on the underworld in general. The ninety-minute series, pulsing, entertaining, and grossly underrated, was seen once a month, sharing a spot with two weeks of movies and another motion-picture transplant, James Stewart as "Hawkins." "Hawkins" was Stewart's second TV show in as many years—coming hard on the heels of a disastrous situation comedy entitled "The Jimmy Stewart Show"—and was his second flop. Stewart played criminal lawyer Billy Jim Hawkins, whose down-home manner and philosophies always got his clients off the hook. Indeed, the only one who seemed to suffer was Stewart, obviously choking over the hurried production schedule of the medium. Meanwhile, more at ease and with a firm, polished grip on every element of his show was the seventy-year-old Buddy Ebsen, who made a hit of the

Buddy Ebsen as Barnaby Jones.

same "aw shucks" character-type in "Barnaby Jones." Jones was a retired private eye who returned to active duty to find the killer of his son Hal (Robert Patton). With the aide of daughter-in-law Betty (Lee Meriwether), he did, in fact, find the killer and decided to stay in business.

With the exception of "Doc Elliot," described by star James Franciscus as "a fellow who comes out of the hustle and bustle of Bellevue Hospital and goes to the Colorado Mountains, where he takes care of miners, hermits, squatters, farmers, and Indians"; "Elephant Boy," starring a young man by the name of Esrem in Sabu's movie role; and "The Starlost," with Keir Dullea as a starship commander probing the universe to gain an understanding of life—the rest of this season belonged to the modern-day lawman. There was Lorne Greene as Wade Griffen, a former Police Captain turned private eye in "Griff"; the excellent and hypnotically authentic omnibus series "Police Story"; "Chase," starring Mitchell Ryan as Capt. Chase Reddick and Wayne Maunder as Det. Sgt. MacCray of the LAPD; and "The Magician," with Bill Bixby as magician Anthony Blake who, after being unjustly convicted of an unmentioned crime, returned to the world-at-large and resolved to use his illusionary skills to help those in need. Shuttling about the country on his private jet plane, Blake was basically a nonviolent crime-fighter: instead of shooting his adversaries, he simply threw doves at them, or made himself disappear.[27]

Discounting "Police Story", these series were all flops, as were the three detective shows created to fill the vacancies in the "NBC Wednesday Mystery Movie": "The Snoop Sisters," a tawdry effort starring Helen Hayes and Mildred Natwick as widows whose hobby was solving crimes; "Faraday and Company," featuring Dan Dailey as Frank Faraday, a detective who joined his son Steve's (James Naughton) practice after having spent twenty-eight years in jail for being wrongly convicted of having killed his partner; and "Tenafly," an excellent series about the not-very-flamboyant Harry Tenafly (James McEachin), a black private eye who worked for Hightower Investigations, Inc. Tenafly took chances regularly, but with great reluctance, and had a home life that ran him ragged. These trappings made "Tenafly" one of the best-delineated dramatic characters in many a television season, with acting that was simply top notch. The sleuth's wife Ruth was portrayed by Lillian Lehman, David Huddleston costarred as Tenafly's boss Lt. Church, and McEachin was a pleasure to watch as our knight in battered armor.

Amidst the carnage of this season's ratings bloodshed,

Kojak (Telly Savalas) confers with guest star Vincent Gardenia.

there emerged three undaunted warriors, two of whom became television powerhouses and one that was cancelled at the star's request after a single season. "Toma" was the one-season entry, the true escapades of Newark, New Jersey, undercover policeman David Toma. Tony Musante starred as the passionate and compassionate hero who usually operated alone and in disguise. And for once, an heroic series came close to portraying, as Toma described himself, "a human being who happens to be a cop." As in "Tenafly," this fleshing-out was accomplished by intruding on the home life of Toma and his wife Patty (Susan Strasberg). It gave

the audience a chance to see the complete man, both at ease and in love, moods that were not only a contrast to the serious, on-the-job Toma, but effected his work through the man himself. They showed that a hero could be a mortal. Costar Simon Oakland as Inspector Spooner also brought out the "human" in Toma, provoking him into fits of rage with his by-the-book ways.

Despite the show's popularity, Musante, as he had said at the onset of "Toma," did not want to be typecast by association with the character and went on to other projects. However, a pair of his fellow actors on the Universal Studios lot had no such reservations about TV,

Telly Savalas as Lt. Theo Kojak.

as "Kojak" and "The Six Million Dollar Man" made superstars of Telly Savalas and Lee Majors. Kojak, as described in a script from the series, "has a face that is an extraordinary mixture of toughness, forged by a life of what he has seen, and gentleness and sensitivity. It is the face of a man in conflict with himself." Whether or not the bald-headed, lollipop-sucking martinet was or was not "in conflict" with himself was moot; but he *was* at war with the rest of the world. He pushed around peers Chief of Detectives Frank McNeil (Dan Frazer), Stavros (Telly's brother, George Demosthenes Savalas), and

plainclothesman Bobby Crocker (Kevin Dobson) as though they were pawns in a chess game; his hatred of punks and crime was so absolute that it superceded his rights as a cop. Theo Kojak didn't hesitate to take a poke at someone who was talking too loud in a restaurant, or rough up an innocent witness at a crime to get information. In short, he was the classic antihero, no different from the crooks that Savalas had played so well in the movies for fifteen years. Now, however, he was operating for the law rather than against it. And his appeal lay in the fact that this was an era of general

140

Lee Majors as the Six Million Dollar Man, in various states of activity.

public dissatisfaction, a time when jobs, Watergate, corrupt politicians, inflation, and generally shoddy service hither and yon had the everyday man down for the count. Kojak was his champion. The policeman's willingness to lash out at hypocrisy and any effort that was not one hundred percent made him a cathartic cult figure to millions of adult viewers. To the kids, however, he was just a grouch, which is why they went for "The Six Million Dollar Man," one of television history's purest heroes. Col. Steve Austin (Lee Majors), an astronaut who was badly mangled in the crash of a test plane, was reassembled by scientists as a *cyborg*, a mechanical human. Austin's robotic or "bionic" elements were a synthetic arm, prosthetic left and right legs both, and a telescopic-infrared eye. These substitutions made Austin a veritable superman who, at first, couldn't have cared less about his powers, and wanted only to be left alone. But the government demanded a return on their six-million-dollar investment and put Austin to work as an undercover agent. Obviously, there was nothing deeper here than good guys versus bad guys, but it, as well as "Kojak," goes to show that if television is neither art or realism, it does at least offer something for seventy million Americans—the combined viewership-per-episode of these two series.

8
Into the Eighties

I'm playing Wonder Woman *as someone who is sensitive, has feelings, and cares about people.*
—*Cathy Lee Crosby, star of the*
first unsold "Wonder Woman" *pilot*

When the trade papers announced, in 1974, that a prehistoric version of "The Waltons" named "Cro-Magnon" was in the works, many people took it to be a joke. Then the series premiered as "Korg," although by now it had become a Saturday-morning children's show. The point is that programers will consider any topic as fodder for a television series. Yet, by and large, they refuse to make dramatic breaks with the past where the hero is concerned. And so, as we near the end of our study, we will find that of the forty-two new adventure and heroic series that were unveiled in 1974–75, the public embraced only nine of them. And of the entire slate, only two shows—one hit and one failure—were somehow inspired by the values and morals of the midseventies.

One of these programs, "The Night Stalker," premiered in 1974. The series was inspired by a pair of made-for-television horror films, "The Night Stalker" and "The Night Strangler,"—both of which were popular attractions in the ratings race. The protagonist in the films and the series both was a moth-eaten reporter by the name of Carl Kolchak (Darren McGavin), who always managed to embroil himself in a story involving monsters: zombies, vampires, and even a beast from the bog. These creatures were never imposters, but were real and utterly ruthless, although never half as ruthless as

Kolchak himself. For one thing, the journalist disregarded the law entirely. If he learned, as he did in one episode, that a fellow passenger on a cruise was a werewolf, due process of the law be damned: Kolchak shot him with a silver bullet. Vampires were staked in the heart. Kolchak also invaded private property and flung accusations at anyone whom he thought might be covering for a monster. Yet beyond these not unusual attributes of the antihero was Kolchak's abrasive

Korg.

Darren McGavin as Carl Kolchak in "The Night Stalker."

manner. While the bulk of his feuding was with editor Vincenzo (Simon Oakland), policemen and government officials would have welcomed any excuse as reason enough to toss the obnoxious reporter in jail. Even the viewer was hard-pressed to tolerate, let alone *like* Kolchak, who blamed everyone for his ill fortune at having fallen from the big-time newsbeat of New York City to contributing penny-ante items to a two-bit tabloid. However, it is significant that he could be so attritive and still exist as the central character in a sixty-minute series, short-lived though it was. Since the element of identification with the down-and-out reporter was almost nil, perhaps we tolerated Kolchak because he boosted our own egos ever so slightly. In any case, there is no denying that he was unique.

Everyone else this season was a hard-working, well-disciplined, and generally virtuous hero of the old school. Actually, hero *and* heroine is a more appropriate designation, since there were seven ladies featured in the 1974 ranks. This, of course, was a radical departure from the male domination of previous years and must be

James Garner of "The Rockford Files."

144

attributed to the growing influence of the various women's movements. Besides a "Wonder Woman" pilot, with its abyssmal update of the classic comic-book heroine, there was Chief of Detectives Amy Prentiss (Jessica Walter), a new member of the "NBC Sunday Mystery Movie" family; "Get Christie Love," starring Teresa Graves as a wisecracking black lady cop, and Charles Cioffi as her boss, Lt. Matthew Reardon; Sally Fergus (Jeanette Nolan) also known as Dirty Sally, a junk dealer who pulled up roots to join ex-outlaw Cyrus Pike (Dack Rambo) on a trek to California; Diana Muldaur and Gary Collins as Joy and George Adamson, the Kenya game wardens of *Born Free*; a Swedish "Waltons" called "The New Land," starring Bonnie Bedelia and Scott Thomas as immigrants Anna and Christian Larsen, who brought their young family to America to settle in Minnesota circa 1860; and "Police Woman," the adventures of Sgt. Pepper Anderson (Angie Dickenson) and Lt. Bill Browley (Earl Holliman). "Police Woman" was the only ratings success of the lot, its strong performances, abundant violence, and emphasis on such subjects as rape and prostitution helping to attract a voyeuristic audience.

As for the men, only James Garner scored a solid hit that season with his new series "The Rockford Files." Garner portrayed Jim Rockford who, in an increasingly popular theme, had spent five years in jail for a crime he didn't commit. Upon his release, the former detective set up shop in a trailer on a California beach and took cases the police were afraid to touch. Lending Jim an occasional hand was his father, Rockford, Sr., played by one of the movies' great character actors, Noah Beery. Among the shakier entries of 1974, but those which nonetheless managed to survive for more than a single season, were David Janssen's "Harry O," San Diego cop Harry Orwell who, with a bullet lodged too near his spine for an operation, still could not resist the lure of crime-fighting and went to work as a private eye; "Petrocelli," starring Barry Newman as the hot-tempered, Harvard-educated Tony Petrocelli, a lawyer in the small Southwestern cow town of San Remo; and "Movin' On," the story of pragmatic truck driver Sonny

David Janssen as "Harry O."

Robert Wagner of "Switch."

Pruett (Claude Akins), his cerebral law-school graduate and partner, Will Chandler (Frank Converse), their thirteen-gear tractor and box, and the trio's adventures on the nation's highways.

Oddly enough, this season's failures were of a particularly colorful nature. For instance, there was "Planet of the Apes," based on the top-grossing five-film series. Everyone in the television industry thought that this was a surefire property, presold as it was and with Roddy McDowall, star of the motion pictures, re-creating his screen role as the chimpanzee Galen. The series was more or less a retelling of the first film as astronauts Virdon (Ron Harper) and Burke (James Naughton) crashed on a world where monkeys were the dominant species and man the inarticulate brute. Yet, despite the presence of the popular ape makeup, bizarre simian-proportioned sets, and generous helpings of action, the series failed. Perhaps it was too much of a good thing.

Back on earth, there were two fast-paced and well-staged flops: "Firehouse," with its weekly format of one small blaze followed by a larger one to confound Capt. Spike Ryerson (James Drury) and Hank Myers (Richard Jaeckel) of Engine Company 23; and "Chopper

One," starring Jim McMullan and Dirk Benedict as airborne officers Don Burdick and Gil Foley who, according to press releases, "patrol their beat over the city at 150 mph!" Meanwhile, protecting the fictitious Sierra National Park were rangers Tim (James G. Richardson), Matt (Ernest Thompson), Jack (Jack Hogan), P. J. (Mike Warner), and Julie (Susan Foster) in Jack Webb's "Sierra"; policing the frigid North for the Alaska State Patrol was Clint Walker as Cal McKay in "Kodiak"; keeping the law in a small New Mexico town was Nakia Parker (Robert Forster), the Navajo deputy sheriff in "Nakia"; serving as a beacon for the misguided students of Harry S. Truman Memorial High School in suburban St. Louis was English teacher and ex-big-league baseball pitcher "Lucas Tanner" (David Hartman); and working as a maskless depression-era "Zorro" was 6'6" Ken Howard as Dave Barrett, a rural farmer who moonlighted as a dread crime-buster in Quinn Martin's "Manhunter." Lastly, there was a television adaptation of John Wayne's 1969 motion picture The Cowboys, as seven adolescent cowhands—Slim (Robert Carradine, David's brother), Cimarron (A. Martinez), Jimmy (Sean Kelly), Weedy (Clay O'Brien), Steve (Clint Howard), Homer (Kerry MacLane), and Hardy (Mitch Brown)—went to work on the ranch of the Widow Anderson (Diana Douglas) under the watchful eyes of foreman Nightlinger (Moses Gunn).

With such an undistinguished season behind him, it's amazing that the television hero was able to rebound and produce seven hits out of the twenty-two programs that premiered in 1975. Of these successes, the moderate hits were "S.W.A.T.," "Switch," "Joe Forrester," and "Ellery Queen."

"S.W.A.T." was the Special Weapons And Tactics police unit headed by Lt. Hondo Harrelson (Steve Forrest) and manned by Sgt. Deacon Kay (Rod Perry), and officers T. J. McCabe (James Coleman) and Dominic Luca (Mark Shera). Naturally, their forte was any situation that the regular police were ill-equipped to handle. "Switch" was also a unique seat of law enforcement, as ex-con Pete Ryan (Robert Wagner) and retired cop Frank MacBride (Eddie Albert) joined forces as private eyes to con criminals. They believed that justice was best served by stealing from other crooks. Then there was "just plain old" "Joe Forrester," starring Lloyd Bridges. Forrester was a veteran cop who watched as time and apathy helped erode his once-proud beat. Thus, when he was offered a safe and quiet desk job, the senior patrolman turned it down, preferring to stay on the streets and help to right wrongs wherever popular. The 1975 season also gave us the third televersion of "Ellery Queen," with Jim Hutton as the 1947 New York-based detective, and David Wayne as his father and partner, Inspector Queen. Violence, cool, humanity, and resourcefulness—these were the respective elements of the heroes in "S.W.A.T.," "Switch," "Joe Forrester," and "Ellery Queen." However, in "Baretta" and "Starsky and Hutch," these four components were meshed to give us a pair of smash hits, one of them excellent and the other not far behind it.

"Baretta," along with "The Night Stalker," was a show that could not have been made in the sixties. "Baretta" was actually a revitalized "Toma," but with a nastier, coarser feel. Tony Baretta (Robert Blake) was an undercover cop and master of disguise who dealt with the underworld in unorthodox fashion. For one thing, Baretta had a network of informers, which included pimps and prostitutes whom he refused to bust. For another, he tended to act not on circumstantial evidence, but on gut reaction. This secretive and personal approach to detective work was a constant source of irritation between Baretta and his superior, Lt. Hal Brubaker (Ed Grover). Brubaker, of course, had to answer to his superiors when, in fact, he often had no idea of what was going on. But he usually gave Baretta reign to work in his mysterious, person-to-person ways. The singular break with "Toma" was that Baretta was a man who liked many women, and thus had no home life of which to speak. He lived in a run-down apartment with a cockatoo named Fred. Yet, his free-wheeling, sensuous way with the ladies told us as much about our hero as did Toma's relationship with Patty. The singular break with tradition was that on "Baretta," it was often difficult to distinguish between the criminals and "the good guys." Each was consumed with self-serving goals, while Baretta was caught in the middle. His prime concern was always, as well it should have been, that society not be the ultimate victim. Thus, despite his unpolished way of speaking, and constant flashes of violent temper against the twin forces pushing at him, Baretta was truly a hero of the public-conscious seventies. Unlike Kojak, who was the vicarious fist and tongue of the harried common man, Baretta was his soul.

"Starsky and Hutch" were a slightly different manner of plainclothes cop—David Starsky (Paul Michael Glaser) being a wise-cracking, gum-chewing, macho-conscious sort, and his partner Ken Hutchinson (David Soul) being more reserved. The men contrasted splendidly with one another, although their chummy patter was sometimes overdone to the point of narcissism. Quizzically, however, while each man was of supreme importance to the other, their treatment of hoods and

Robert Blake as Baretta.

gangsters was barbaric. Indeed, the only complaint that one can rightfully lodge against the show is that the violence was overstated, often reminding the viewer of the ribald fights once staged for "Batman." Of course, where there's a "Batman" there's a "Batgirl": in this case it was the season's third blockbuster, "The Bionic

Woman." Lindsay Wagner was featured as a lady *cyborg* in this companion series to the Lee Majors opus.

However, 1975 was not all roses for the ladies. The six-million-dollar woman struck ratings gold, as did the four-episode "Wonder Woman" effort, starring Lynda Carter as the original Wonder Woman, complete with a

Starsky and Hutch pose as pimps . . .

Robert Blake and Fred of "Baretta."

. . . and as they normally are.

Lindsay Wagner as Jaime Sommers, the Bionic Woman.

The Bionic Woman.

colorful costume, Amazonian heritage, and Lyle Waggoner as love interest Col. Steve Trevor. Unfortunately, lawyer "Kate McShane," a mere mortal, wasn't as lucky. Despite enthusiastic and sincere performances by Anne Meara in the title role, Sean McClory as her policeman father, and Charles Haid as her brother Eddie, a Jesuit priest, the show was gone by midseason. The remaining casualties, not limited to a single sex or religion, were "Caribe," with Stacy Keach and Carl Franklin as Miami cops Ben Logan and Mark Walters who operated in the Caribbean; "Bronk," cocreated by "All in the Family's" Carroll O'Connor and starring Jack Palance as Alexander Bronkov, a tough but soft-spoken plainclothesman; "Matt Helm," featuring Tony Franciosa as the detective

Jack Palance as Bronk. That's an harmonica he's holding in his left hand.

Tony Curtis in disguise for "McCoy."

Jackie Cooper (right) and aide in "Mobile One."

Doug McClure (left) and William Shatner of "The Barbary Coast."

George Kennedy as Bumper Morgan in "The Blue Knight," a series based on the Joseph Wambaugh novel.

whose world was stocked with lovely ladies, a flurry of dangerous assignments, and plenty of advice from his lawyer and confidant Ms. Kronski (Laraine Stephens); Jack Webb's "Mobile One," starring Jackie Cooper as Pete Campbell, a newsman assigned to a TV mobile unit; and "NBC Sunday Mystery Movie" entry "McCoy," starring Tony Curtis as a gambler and con man. The more exotic fizzles were Irwin Allen's "Swiss Family Robinson," based on the classic Johann Wyss novel about a family shipwrecked on an uncharted island; "The Invisible Man," in which Daniel Westin (David McCallum) rendered himself transparent and went to work for a government agent played by Craig Stevens; and "Barbary Coast," with William Shatner and Doug McClure. Set in San Francisco of the 1880s, the series starred McClure as Cash Conover, owner of a gambling casino that served as the inauspicious front for the luxurious residence of government undercover agent Jeff Cable (Shatner). There were also a pair of medical washouts this season, as the excellent anthology "Medical Story" was cancelled, along with "Doctor's Hospital," in which George Peppard played the brusque Jim Goodwin, chief of

Would-be heroes. Pictured are the mortal assistants of the "Super Friends," a kid's show featuring the exploits of Superman, Aquaman, Wonder Woman, etc. Cartoons intended for consumption in the Saturday-morning time slots are generally poorly written and always drawn and animated with the utmost economy.

One of the better Saturday morning children's shows within recent memory has been "Shazam!" Pictured is Jackson Bostwick as the superpowered Captain Marvel.

neurosurgery at Lowell Memorial Hospital.

As of this writing, the 1976 season has proven almost as disastrous. Midseason replacements for the above-mentioned September 1975 flops met with an unsympathetic public, as Harold "Oddjob" Sakata's Det. "Khan," Brian Keith's Det. "Archer," and Wayne Rogers' Det. Jake Axminster in "City of Angels" were abandoned. The fate of George Kennedy's excellent police drama "The Blue Knight," Jack Warden's "Jigsaw John," David Birney's "Serpico," and the stunt flier drama "Spencer's Pilots" were equally cataclysmic. Only the coy, abysmally acted Kate Jackson, Farrah Fawcett-Majors, Jaclyn Smith series "Charlie's Angels" —Charlie being off-screen operative John Forsythe— has shown any staying power, zooming to the top of the ratings charts due to its lack of clothing rather than its abundance of talent. As with "Sheena," women are still being presented as sexual playthings rather than as human beings capable of entertaining any serious

Joining "Shazam!" in 1975, for its second season, was the goddess Isis.

154

Proving that you can go from bad to worse, the "Planet of the Apes" live-action series failure was followed by "Return to the Planet of the Apes," a Saturday-morning cartoon series. Pictured are astronauts Judy Franklin, Jeff Carter, and Bill Hudson.

Wonder Woman as she was seen on Super Friends.

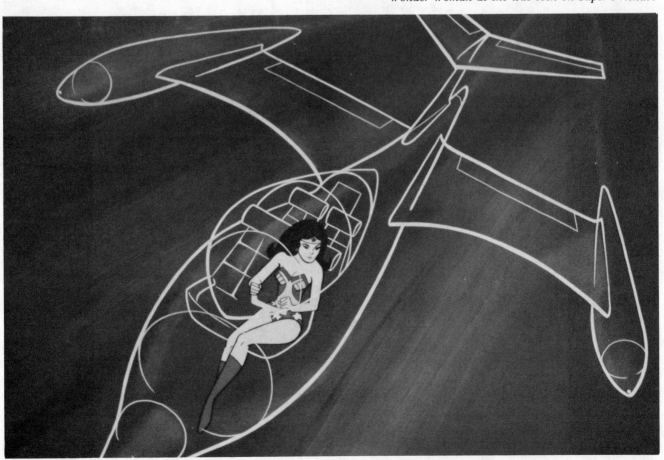

Aquaman.

One-shot antihero. Paul Shenar as Orson Welles in the ABC
made for television film "The Night the Martians Landed"
(1975).

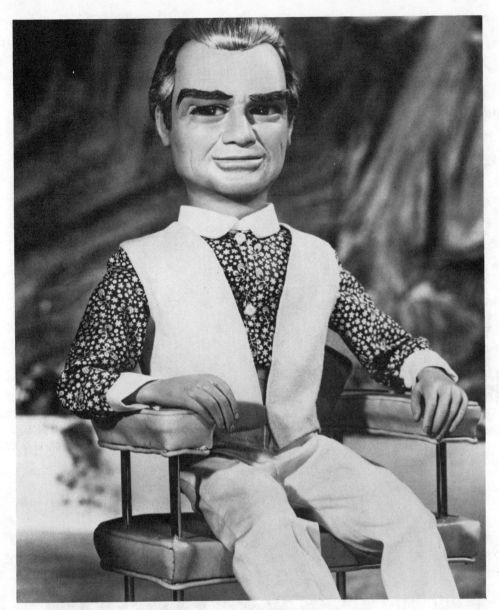

One of the marionettes seen in "Thunderbird Six," a children's show in the tradition of Fireball XL-5. These marionette shows have proved extremely popular, other such entries being "Capt. Scarlet" and "Super Car." They were created by the Gerry and Sylvia Anderson team, the same group responsible for the live-action "UFO" and "Space: 1999" series.

This is Superman? Actually, it's Clark Kent (David Wilson) who cowers before the advances of Sydney Carlton (Loretta Swit) in a poor adaptation of the hit Broadway musical Superman. Superman was seen on ABC's "Wide World of Entertainment" in February, 1975.

The cast of "Happy Days." Although he is not a hero in our consideration of the term, Henry Winkler's character Fonzie (second from right) has built a huge cult following.

Gabriel Kaplan as Kotter in the comedy series "Welcome Back Kotter." Like Fonzie, the high-school students in Kotter's classroom—called the Sweathogs—have become cult heroes.

If Fonzie and the Kotter "Sweathog" teenagers represent free-wheeling heroes for the young, then Archie Bunker (Carroll O'Connor) is a beleaguered hero to Middle America in "All in the Family." The bigoted Archie—shown here with daughter Gloria (Sally Struthers) on her wedding day—cannot understand that all men and women have the same rights as American citizens that he does. Archie is a classic antihero: he does what's right for him regardless of whoever else his action effects.

"Charlie's Angels."

From "Charlie's Angels."

thoughts. Hopefully, that primitive, uninformed attitude will one day be abandoned. Other entries, late in 1976 and early in 1977, were the detective program "Delvecchio"; the water-breathing "Man from Atlantis" starring Patrick Duffy, Belinda Montgomery, and Art Lund; James Franciscus's "Hunter," about a government intelligence unit; Ernest Borgnine's "Future Cop," the tale of a policeman and his robot partner; and the Coast Guard drama "Code R."

As future seasons get underway, the reader can be certain of several things. Fundamentally, the hero will be no different than he or she has been through the years. They may walk around bra-less, like they do in "Charlie's Angles," as the vehicles change to reflect contemporary mores. But the characters will all be heroes, survivors, or anti-heroes. There will be special product geared to children and minority groups, as well as for the general public: it will be tailored to provide us with the various personal heroes that we need. In this respect, as we said in our Introduction, television is an intimate tool, creating a desirable reality that it brings into our homes. And when full-size, 3-D television becomes commonplace in the eighties, who knows? TV might then ask us to participate in its fare, making heroes of the viewers themselves.

We look forward to seeing you ten years hence with a volume discussing the pros and cons of such a medium!

"Wonder Woman."

Notes

1. The networks, of course, are ABC, CBS, and NBC. They have affiliate stations in every major city—stations that show most network produced fare. When these network or "web" presentations finish their run, they are sold to independent stations the nation and world over, where they are rerun as long as there is an audience.

2. It has been traditional that kids follow the examples of good- and clean-living established by heroes. This has been particularly so in the twentieth century, where the heroes who appeared in pulp magazines and comic books went so far as to publish their standards for right behavior.

3. Prime time is a period of the evening when television is most watched. Its hours are traditionally 7:30 to 11:00 P.M.

4. It should be remembered that at this time, most stations were losing money. It was 250% more expensive to run a television station as opposed to a radio station, so programers were anxious to come up with fare that would get them out of the red.

5. Ironically, "Capt. Video" proved so popular that it became a movie serial shortly after the TV series premiered. Judd Holdren played Video in the fifteen-chapter Columbia effort.

6. In 1953, *TV Digest* was sold to its present owners, and changed its name from *TV Digest and Guide* to *TV Guide* within a matter of weeks.

7. After nearly forty years of not having received a penny from their multimillion-dollar creation, Siegel and Schuster were awarded $20,000 per year token payments by the character's current owner, Warner Communications.

8. In addition to a stunning wardrobe, Autry owned the 290-acre Melody Ranch, on which he raised horses and grew walnuts and fruit.

9. In 1935, Gene Autry inaugurated the practice of stars using their own names in movies. Thus, in "Tumbling Tumbleweeds," it was Gene Autry as himself, rather than Gene Autry as John Doe.

10. On the radio, Steve Wilson was played by Edward G. Robinson.

11. A rhetorical question: Why is it that in most of the movies and TV series of the thirties, forties, and fifties, we never saw a cowboy doing that for which he was named, namely, minding cattle?

12. It's truly amazing how the Capitol Building was visible from every window in video's re-creation of Washington D.C. What's even more astounding is how, in one show—which shall be nameless to protect its already fleeting fame—the Capitol was seen through the window of—the Capitol!

13. Daly left the show, incidentally, because he was homesick. In fact, so blinded was he by longing that he was heard to complain "there aren't as many pretty girls on location as there are on one block in Hollywood or New York."

14. It should be pointed out that many stars wanted to produce their own shows in order to coordinate the merchandising of characters. One of the most popular toys of this era, for example, was a Ramar board game, which reaped considerable profits for Hall's organization.

15. There is a telling footnote on the irony of the heroic image. One of the West's great hero-makers is Rodd Redwing. A Chickasaw Indian, he taught both Clayton Moore and Gail Davis how to handle their guns like experts. And yet, he was forced to remain anonymous. According to Redwing, "Sometimes I'm asked to sign a paper agreeing not to disclose that I've worked with someone, as some people believe it would destroy the illusions involved."

16. When Dillon moved into Dodge City, Earp moved out and into Tombstone. Historicity is great—as long as it doesn't interfere with drama.

17. Like Paladin, Boone himself lived by standards unusual for the time. For one thing, in an era when actors were coming out for this political candidate or that, Boone contributed to Kennedy's campaign but refused to support him in terms of personal appearances. He felt this was an unfair influence on voters. Second, Boone made personal appearances where he felt they would do some good; in hospitals, for example. On one visit to a rehabilitation center for retarded children, he handed out his Wire Paladin cards, telling one youngster, "If you ever get into any trouble around here, send me one of those and I'll come and straighten it out." An eyewitness said several nurses fought back tears of gratitude for the joy Boone brought the children.

18. In addition to mocking the general Western image, "Maverick" took a number of pot shots at television. In their spoof of "The Untouchables," Lancelot Vest came West and battled Frank Nifty, Capt. Scarface, Slugs Moran, and Jake Gooseneck. For the "Bonanaza" grilling, the gamblers faced Moose, Small Paul, and Henry of the Wheelright family.

19. One of "Wagon Train's" episodes was actually a pilot for Bette Davis' proposed but unsold series "Madame's Place."

20. Ness was so incorruptible that even when he posed as a criminal, his alias nearly gave him away: who would have believed that Whitey Steele was an underworld figure?

21. Something else with which heroes wrestled were the titles of their programs. One episode of "Straightaway" was called "Nobles Oblige"; "Tightrope" went so far as to air an effort entitled "Achilles and His Heels."

22. Raich, of course, was really a one-armed man. Surprisingly, he made a good living in the movies, especially in epics: he was always the Roman soldier who, in full view of the camera and wearing a false limb, had his arm cut off during a battle. The one such scene of which he was most proud, in *Spartacus* (1960), ended up on the cutting-room floor. It was deemed too bloody for the public.

23. So thrilled with the series was Hoover that he once said, "I have received hundreds of letters from people saying that Efrem Zimbalist, Jr.'s inspector and the *FBI* series, portrayed what they thought FBI agents should portray. I want our own agents to live up to that image." With recent revelations about the bureau's covert activities regarding Martin Luther King and other private citizens being what they are, we can only wish that life had imitated art more closely.

24. Two "Star Trek" pilots were necessary to sell the series to NBC. The first one starred Jeffrey Hunter as the captain of the Enterprise. The pilot with Hunter was later seen—with a new framing story—as the two-part "Menagerie" episode.

25. For trivia fans, there was also a continuing character in "Congressional Investigator" called Dan August.

26. Like the "Dr. Kildare-Eleventh Hour" experiment before it, there were also "Marcus Welby-Owen Marshall" crossovers.

27. As an interesting aside, all of the magic seen in "The Magician" was performed by Bixby under the tutelage of the world-renowned Mark Wilson. Special camera tricks were never employed.

Index

171

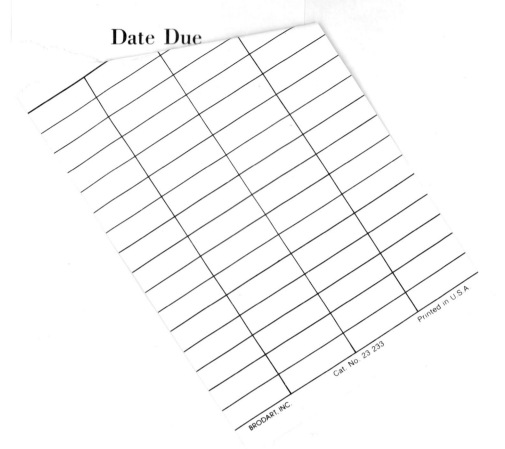

Date Due

BRODART, INC.

Cat. No. 23 233

Printed in U.S.A.